BOOKS by ED DEVOS

The Stain
The Chaplains Cross
Revenge at Kings Mountain
Family of Warriors

BOOKS by BOB BABCOCK

War Stories Volumes I: Utah Beach to Liberation of Paris
War Stories Volume II: Paris to VE Day
War Stories Volume III: Vietnam 1968 to 1970
What Now, Lieutenant?
Operation Iraqi Freedom I: A Year in the Sunni Triangle
Operation Iraqi Freedom 07-09: Dispatches from Baghdad
With Honor We Served
I'm Ready to Talk
You Don't Know Jack ... or Jerry
World War II WAC with Helen Denton as told to Bob Babcock

THE LAST
100 YARDS

THE LAST 100 YARDS

HOW THE INFANTRY PROJECTS POWER & STRENGTH AROUND THE GLOBE

Ed DeVos

Deeds Publishing | Athens

Published by Deeds Publishing in Athens, GA
www.deedspublishing.com

Printed in The United States of America

Cover design by Mark Babcock.

ISBN 978-1-950794-17-1

Books are available in quantity for promotional or premium use. For information, email info@deedspublishing.com.

First Edition, 2020

10 9 8 7 6 5 4 3 2 1

This book is dedicated to all those who have served, are serving, and will one day serve in the Infantry. Colonel Ralph Puckett, USA (Ret) inspired the title of this book when he stated that:

"The Last 100 yards ... is the ... most dangerous piece of land on the globe."

CONTENTS

Introduction   xi
The Infantryman's Creed   xiii
Acknowledgements   xv

1. Congratulations, Lieutenant   1
2. Fort Benning, Georgia. The First Time   17
3. 509th Airborne Infantry. Mainz Germany. A Period of Maturing   35
4. Vietnam. The "Quiet" Time   51
5. Vietnam. The 1972 NVA Easter Offensive   69
6. Fort Benning, Georgia. On the Road to Professionalism   95
7. Fort Benning, Georgia. Days of Learning   103
8. Furman University, Greenville, SC. Building a Legacy   121
9. V Corps, Frankfurt, Germany. A Period of Growth   133
10. Fort Leavenworth, Kansas. Mission Accomplished.   145
11. Fort Ord, California. The First Two Years.   155
12. Fort Ord, California. The Chief of Staff's Dream   171
13. Fort Drum, New York. Train Up and Activation   189
14. Fort Drum, New York. Climbing to the Top   199
15. The Last Farewell   219

Epilogue   227
Abbreviations   231

About the Author   235

INTRODUCTION

In the last few years I have met a number of men and women who express a significant yearning in their hearts; a deep desire to know what their father or brother or son or uncle did while they wore one of the uniforms of the Armed Forces of our country. In many cases, the ex-service member simply did not want to talk about his experiences in the service, and so as these ex-service members grew older, they eventually passed on. On that day, a piece of our nation's history was buried with them, never to see the light of day.

Part of me understands why these veterans chose not to share their experiences. Perhaps their memories were too horrific or horrible and it seemed better to them to spare their loved ones any details because of the veteran's affection for their loved ones. Another part of me hears the families who are left behind, and their desire to know what "Dad" did, or saw, or felt because of their love and respect for him. From the families' perspective, by not knowing what "Dad" lived through, they realize part of their family legacy will never be known, will never be shared, and will never be honored.

I, too, as an old soldier wrestled with this dilemma, and after much deliberation, I have chosen to tell something about my twenty years as an Infantry soldier, and pass it to my children and my grandchildren and to any others who wish to know more of the history of our country. It was not an easy decision as my mind played some tricks with me about some of the good and bad times, but nevertheless, what follows are my recollections of some of my days in the service of our country. Errors in dates and locations and some minute details are mine, and mine alone. Some names have been changed to protect those who cannot defend themselves as my impressions of them may not be flattering. To do anything else would be unfair to them.

So here is my story of seventy-three-hundred days in the United States Army. As a youngster, some called me Eddie, which I did not particularly like. As I grew older, I was called Ed by most outside the family. To my mother and father, I was always Ed, Jr. To avoid a great number of "I's" and "my's", this paper is written in third person. I trust that will assist you in reading the pages that follow.

THE INFANTRYMAN'S CREED

I am the Infantry
I am my country's strength in war, her deterrent in peace.
I am the heart of the fight...whenever, wherever.
I carry America's faith and honor against her enemies.
I am the Queen of Battle.
I am what my country expects me to be, the best trained Soldier in the world.
In the race for victory, I am swift, determined, and courageous,
Armed with a fierce will to win.
Never will I fail my country's trust.
Always I fight on...through the foe, to the objective, to triumph overall.
If necessary, I will fight to my death.
By my steadfast courage, I have won more than 200 years of freedom.
I yield to no weakness, to hunger, to cowardice, to fatigue, to superior odds,
For I am mentally tough, physically strong, and morally straight.
I forsake not, my country, my mission, my comrades, my scared duty.
I am relentless. I am always there, now and forever.

I AM THE INFANTRY! FOLLOW ME!

ACKNOWLEDGEMENTS

Publication of any book is a team effort. While the authors give birth to the ideas, for this book many others provided information, facts, remembrances, direction, and grounding. Others provide the fine tuning, helping me, in particular, to stay within the lines of the language. The members of the Deeds Publishing team, a first-rate organization, provided the technical expertise to pull everything together in the proper format, the cover art, and the actual publication of the book. Thank you.

Among the list of unsung heroes that contributed to this effort are military veterans LTC Paul Griffith, (USA Retired), Ron Male, COL Mike Pasquarett (USA Retired), LTC "Buzz" Sherwood (USA Retired), COL Dave Pate (USA Retired), COL Pete Dillon (USA Retired), LTC Mike Eggers (USA Retired), and COL Ken Sampson (Chaplain, USA Retired). Two others of special note who helped with their sharp eyes were Dr. Charles Lewis (Chaplain, LTC, USAF Retired) and Mrs. Joan Prince. Our wives, Susan DeVos and Jan Babcock also played crucial roles as they patiently allowed us to work on this project without interruption.

The heart and soul of this book is the Infantry soldier. Bob and I were both privileged to serve with these soldiers and so this book is dedicated to all Infantrymen, to those whose mission it is to close with and destroy the enemy in the last 100 yards — the most dangerous piece of land on the globe. We cannot say enough about those men. We hope you will also have a better appreciation for all those who serve in our nation's military for the sacrifice—not only the service member, but the spouses and their children as well. What these families deal with on a day-to-day basis gives new meaning to the phrase, 'Freedom is not Free.'

—**Ed DeVos & Bob Babcock**

1. CONGRATULATIONS, LIEUTENANT

"Congratulations, Lieutenant," the smiling Sergeant Major said as he saluted United States Army 2nd Lieutenant Edward G. DeVos Jr. on that beautiful day in May 1969.

DeVos saluted and then reached into his pants pocket, pulling out a brand new dollar bill and put it in the outstretched hand of the man who had just honored him by rendering this brand new infantry officer with all of five minutes in grade his first salute. The NCO of over twenty-five years of service held the young officer's hand for a second or two longer than necessary as he gave this twenty-two year old a brief nod of encouragement. In that moment, it seemed to DeVos that the torch was being passed from one generation to the next.

It had been a good day: graduating from Florida Southern College and receiving his commission in the U.S. Army through the college's Reserve Officers' Training Corps (ROTC) program. For the rest of the day, many memories flooded his brain as he and Susan packed what little they had in their renovated two-car garage apartment two blocks from campus into a small U-Haul trailer that was hitched behind their car. Then they were off. Their next stop was four hundred miles north: Columbus, Georgia and the home of the United States Army Infantry Center, Fort Benning.

Because he was a Distinguished Military Graduate (DMG), this brand new Second Lieutenant (2LT) was immediately appointed as a Regular Army Officer, equivalent to those who would be commissioned near this time at West Point. So what did all that mean? Where would it take them? There was excitement mixed with much uncertainty, and yes, to some degree with some fear and trepidation. But with the confidence of the young who know just enough to be dangerous, their journey began. Oh the memories...

* * * * *

Ed thought his growing up years were much like all the other kids he knew. From his perspective, he judged his parents to be the best in the world, giving him the appropriate amount of guidance, but not too much; surrounding him with unconditional love without smothering the daylights out of him; teaching him the value of a dollar; and modeling their Christian morals and values which formed a solid foundation for his beliefs and standards that still have great meaning for him today. Most importantly, they allowed him freedom to make some mistakes along the way, believing that experience can be one of life's best teachers.

The DeVos', like their friends and those they associated with, lived through the ups and downs of World War II. Ed Sr. was a bombardier in B-24s in the Pacific Theater where he flew forty combat missions in the 307th Bombardment Group (Heavy). On one of these missions, he and those with him were awarded a Presidential Unit Citation. Ed Jr.'s mother, Dorothy, helped her mother and father throughout the war, putting food on the table by planting a Victory Garden and earning money by working in her father's radio repair shop. During this time she became an accomplished pianist, an enjoyment of hers that remained for the rest of her life. One of Dorothy's brothers, Jay, who died in 1995, was a tank commander in North Africa in the 1st Armored Division. Wounded in combat, he had five tanks shot out from under him, received a battlefield commission, and was awarded the Silver Star for gallantry in battle.

Soon after Ed Sr. returned from the Pacific, he and Dorothy married in May 1945 in front of one hundred and thirty witnesses at Fifth Reformed Church in Grand Rapids, Michigan, and soon after that, he turned down the opportunity to stay in the Army Air Corps and get promoted immediately to the rank of Major. While he continued to serve his country in the Air Force Reserves for another seven years, he never second-guessed his decision to leave active duty.

After honeymooning in Santa Ana, California, the young couple settled back in Grand Rapids, a growing metropolis in southwestern Michigan, known by many as "Furniture City." When the war ended, Ed Sr. began applying his skills in woodworking, a trade he had learned from his father, which led to him opening a business that focused on making and installing fine cabinetry. His business grew quickly as his reputation for excellent work spread.

In April 1947, Ed Jr. was born. Early photographs attest to his interest in airplanes and the construction industry as evidenced by the toy airplanes and blocks that were always present. This attraction to construction tools caused a problem one day when this rambunctious two-year old picked up a hammer and proceeded to put a rather large hole in a newly installed bathtub in his parent's bathroom.

In 1950 a business opportunity came to Ed Sr.'s attention, the possibilities of which were so good, he and Dorothy decided to move fourteen hundred miles from Grand Rapids to Lake Worth, Florida, a town of 10,000 on the Atlantic Ocean bordering West Palm Beach to the north. Palm Beach, the home of the rich and famous, was right across the intra-coastal river on the Atlantic Ocean. There, Ed Sr. became the foreman for his brother's construction company which was just beginning to reap the benefits of a growing south Florida.

In the years that followed, DeVos Construction Company grew

significantly as the company went from concentrating on building houses in the booming market to focusing more on building larger structures
such as churches, office buildings, and schools. Meanwhile, Dorothy, not
one to sit on her hands for too long, decided to start a toy store business in downtown Lake Worth. After running that business for several
years, she took a position as the school secretary of Highland Elementary School in Lake Worth. Two of the students in that school were a set
of twins: Susan and Katherine Bentley.

Ed Jr.' growing up years were much like those he palled around with.
Since Lake Worth was a fairly small and quiet town, it was not unusual
that on Saturday mornings, he and his friends would walk six blocks to
go to the movie theater downtown or walk the ten blocks to go fish-
ing for toad fish and red snapper along the seawall of the intra-coastal
waterway. In the sixth grade, at age twelve, he was selected to be the
head of the student school patrol guiding carpooling mothers to areas
where they could drop off their children on the school grounds. Later
that year, like many other school patrol members at the local schools in
Palm Beach County, he was given the opportunity to travel from Florida
to Washington, D.C by train and tour the nation's capital for four or five
days, all chaperoned, of course.

His grades through these years of grade school were above average,
although one teacher commented that he always wanted to answer all
the questions in his class, thereby giving no one else a chance to give
their thoughts. Having received that counsel, the boy backed away from
school work a bit and pursued with increased vigor his first love: sports.
To his advantage, the DeVos' lived one block from the school and so all
the ball fields and courts were available every day of the week and after
school as well. Also, his older cousins lived across the street, and the
two boys, Doug and Mike, were high school varsity athletes, who, from
time-to-time, gave Ed Jr. the opportunity to play ball with them in their
pickup games. This gave him the chance to learn valuable skills from the

older boys, although Ed Sr. was always ready to play catch after he got home from work.

These opportunities led to him playing on a Little League baseball team for three years and culminated in pitching a no-hitter and making the All-Star team for the area. Some of his efforts to excel at sports were hampered a bit because during this time when it was discovered he needed glasses. In the years that followed, he wore contact lenses in high school, and after losing a number of contact lens on football fields and basketball courts around Palm Beach County, he was fitted for athletic contacts which solved that problem. He continued to wear contacts up into his early 30's.

Ed Jr.' first began to earn some money by receiving a weekly allowance for doing chores around the house: keeping his room in good order, mowing the grass, trimming the bushes, sweeping the sidewalk, and washing and drying all the dishes after supper every night. At age eleven, he decided to start selling Christmas cards door-to-door and also delivering the weekly TV Guides to the neighborhood for sixteen cents a copy, earning four cents for each sale. His motivation for these efforts was to surprise his mother at Christmas with a gift of an electric griddle which would be purchased with money he earned.

Another significant event happened around this same time-frame as in his seventh grade in English, he began to play "footsies" with this cute girl named Susan Bentley. That "puppy love" continues to grow and grow to this day.

One of the pivotal moments in this young man's life occurred when he attended a Methodist Youth Camp near Leesburg, Florida in the summer of 1960. While the three-day camp was invigorating and filled with a number of outdoors activities—swimming, archery, walks in the woods to look at wildlife in all its forms—early one evening, this thirteen-year-old was moved to take a walk by himself to the nearby lake, and as he was there, he spent a long time gazing at a well-lit cross placed

5

at the water's edge. It was there that his heart was stirred to believe that he wanted Jesus Christ to be the Lord of his life. While he never told anyone too much about that early evening at the lake, from that moment on, Ed felt that Jesus was watching over him, protecting him, guiding him. It is a scene that has never left him although sadly, nothing really changed in his attendance in church or other church activities for a number of years.

At age sixteen in 1963, Ed Jr. started working for DeVos Construction Company as a laborer and worked every summer as well as during all the school breaks through graduation from college. He learned to handle a shovel and a lot of other tools as he dug a lot of ditches, carried a lot of concrete blocks, tied a lot of steel, pushed a great number of wheelbarrows, and pounded a lot of nails from the towns of Stuart in the north to Delray Beach in the south and out to Belle Glade, Pahokee, and Canal Point near Lake Okeechobee to the west. The most unique construction project he helped with was pouring concrete into the wooden forms to make the concrete and steel walls of a bank vault in Lantana, Florida. His starting pay at sixteen was a $1.35 an hour before taxes.

To help build up some additional cash, the young man found a second job at night as the official score keeper and announcer for the Little League baseball games at the same field where he had played years earlier. The pay was one dollar per game plus ice cream from the snack store underneath the press box where he did his announcing. Since she lived close to the ball field, that girl, Susan, joined him in the press box on a number of nights, as he shared some of his ice cream with her. Because he now had a little more money, Ed Jr. asked his father, who invested some of his dollars with a stockbroker, if he could tag along with his dad one day to meet this man. After studying some material and several business magazines, this seventeen-year old made his first investment in stock in the New York Stock Exchange.

High school was a good time for the son of Ed and Dorothy. He studied all the sciences — Earth Science, Biology, Chemistry, and Physics — all the mathematics to include Algebra, Calculus, and Geometry, World and U.S. history, four years of English, Government, Latin for three years, and, of course, Physical Education. Most days after school were filled with practicing and playing football in the fall and golf in spring, a sport he had been introduced to by his parents when he was twelve.

While his golf game was improving each year, he concentrated more on football, which led to him being awarded the Unsung Hero award for the Lake Worth High School Football Team in his senior year for his consistent play as an offensive lineman, defensive linebacker, and the long snapper for punts, extra points, and field goal tries. During the season opener his senior year, he showed true grit by playing the entire game on two badly infected ankles which earned him a five-day hospital stay to get the infection out of his system. While he received several letters from colleges and universities requesting film so they could evaluate his football abilities, one hundred and seventy-pound linemen were not going to be taken too seriously by even the small colleges. It was, however, a thrill to be invited to a gathering of Princeton University hopefuls one evening at a plush hotel in Palm Beach.

Golf, on the other hand, offered some better possibilities. He made his first hole-in-one his senior year of high school, but if the truth were told about that shot, it was a worm burner that just happened to end up in the hole. A perfect example of, "Sometimes it's better to be lucky than good." Because of his potential, Ed and Dorothy blessed a trip one summer for young Ed and three other seventeen-year old guys to drive to play in two junior golf tournaments on the west coast of Florida, one hundred and fifty miles away. These four teenagers were there for six days on their own playing golf. While Ed played okay, some fifteen-year old kid from the Fort Worth, Texas area won both tournaments. Name was Kite. Tom Kite. Years later this man won the U.S. Open at Pebble Beach and is now in the World Golf Hall of Fame.

* * * * *

Ed Jr. was the first person in his family to attend college. While there were several possibilities open to him, at his mother's urging, he decided to go to Florida Southern College (FSC), a Methodist-sponsored liberal arts college in Lakeland, Florida. Since his family worshipped in a Methodist church, Dorothy felt strongly about this course of action, and in retrospect, it was a good fit. FSC was a small school of fifteen hundred located on the northern shores of Lake Hollingsworth on the south side of Lakeland. Besides a solid reputation for academics, it was known for having several buildings on campus designed by the famous architect Frank Lloyd Wright.

Fundamental to FSC's approach to higher education was that each student get a broad education in the first two years before focusing on a specific major and a minor the last two years. In that regard, Ed could expect in his freshman and sophomore years to attend classes in English, mathematics, science, a foreign language of his choosing, world and U.S. history, introductory courses in religions of the world, art and music appreciation, physical fitness, and military science (ROTC). In addition to these academic requirements, each Wednesday morning there was "convocation," a two-hour lecture from world-renown figures speaking on various subjects ranging from politics to science to economics to business and other topics of general interest. Among the speakers that came to FSC during Ed's college years were Vice-President Hubert Humphrey, the South African Doctor, Christiaan Barnard, the man who performed the world's first human heart transplant, and the Army Chief of Staff, General Harold K. Johnson.

DeVos was in some advanced classes in his first semester of college in the fall of 1965 and found that, while being in the top third in his high school class was a confidence builder, he was now fighting to stay in the middle third of his classes in college. Quite a wake-up call to find out that he wasn't as smart as he thought he was. As a pre-med major who harbored dreams of being a brain surgeon one day, what had come so easily in high school was not the case as a college freshman. To make matters worse, he almost got kicked out of college his first semester for getting involved in a silly, dumb prank, but thanks to a "somewhat" understanding dean, this repentant freshman was given a second chance and he made the most of it.

With this increased maturity, DeVos buckled down, getting his grades closer to where they should be. In Ed's second semester of his freshman year, he pledged to a fraternity, Tau Kappa Epsilon (TKE), joining men with names like Warren, Lesher, Bremer, Honeycutt, Edinger, Phillips, Denmark, Downard, Cobb, and many others. He also changed his major to Business with a minor in Economics, which was a much better fit for his talents, academic abilities, and interests. With his above average athletic ability, he became quite involved in all the fraternity intramurals—flag football, basketball, softball, and in a one-time attempt at intramural wrestling, a sport he had never seen, much less tried, but when his fraternity brothers called he said "put me in." His opponent for that first match was a fellow from one of TKE's biggest rivals who was the Ohio State High School Wrestling Champion in his weight class. Within thirty seconds (it seemed more like ten), Ed was doing his best impression of a being a pretzel, flat on his back, pinned, his wrestling career came to an abrupt halt.

More rewarding fraternity activities followed, including paddling down the calm Peace River on sunny Saturday afternoons trying to grab beer cans as they floated in the water, or "Greek" sing competitions against other fraternities, collecting gifts for needy kids of Lakeland around holiday time, or picking oranges off the trees in the orange grooves in the winter to help beleaguered farmers before a severe frost killed their crops.

Because FSC was a land-grant college, ROTC was mandatory for the first two years for all male students, and with its long history of supporting this program, FSC had quite a legacy of commissioning students into the U.S. Army upon graduation. From that first Wednesday afternoon drill, Ed found that he fit right into the concept of service to the country and the entire flavor of the program. Within two weeks, he volunteered to be a member of the "Guerrilla Platoon," a group who would be the "aggressors" against the senior ROTC cadets on exercises that would take place once or twice each semester. Two weeks later, he was one of twenty members of the Guerrilla Platoon that participated in an overnight exercise at Drane Field, an airfield just to the south of Lakeland that had been used in World War II to train Army Air Corps bomber crews and fighter pilots. During this first venture in the field, this young soldier-to-be learned the importance of always carrying toilet paper with you when you go out into the woods for any length of time.

The next exercise he participated in was a month later at Avon Park Bombing Range fifty miles southeast of FSC. This exercise began on campus as UH-1 Huey helicopters swooped in and landed at the water's edge of Lake Hollingsworth to pick up the Guerrilla Platoon right in front of the college's "sorority row" and flew these officers-to-be right into the exercise area where they walked all night through a thick, dark, tangled mangrove swamp to surprise the "enemy" early the next morning. To add to the excitement, the platoon was flown back to campus later that morning, reeking of swamp smells. To the delight of the coeds, these guerrillas then marched past them on their way to the ROTC building to turn in equipment.

Each week was another adventure; firing the M-1 rifle one week and then the M-14 the next; practicing marksmanship in the basement of the ROTC building, drilling and doing PT every Wednesday afternoon, all while hearing more each day about the United States' Armed Forces involvement in South Vietnam.

* * * * *

Between studying, ROTC, and fraternity life, Ed still made time to drive the two hundred miles to Lake Worth once a month to seriously court that girl Susan. One of his fraternity brothers was a key enabler in this endeavor as he loaned Ed his car, a GTO, the big muscle car of that day, once a month to make those trips back and forth. On those weekend visits, Ed would arrive in Lake Worth early Friday night and drive back to Lakeland early Monday morning for an 8 AM class. As this relationship grew, Ed gave Susan his fraternity lavaliere and then his fraternity pin, all signs pointing toward life-long happiness.

During the summer between their sophomore and junior years of college, Ed, after careful planning, approached Susan's father early one evening to ask for her hand in marriage. Her dad, who was sitting on a couch after a hard day of work at his landscaping business, relaxing in a T-shirt and shorts, sized the young man up for a moment or two before he smiled as he got up from the couch and said, "Excuse me. I'll be right back." After what seemed like an hour, Susan's father walked back into the room with a tie fully knotted over his T-shirt. Staring wisely at the nervous young man, he asked, "Now what would you like to talk about?"

Later that evening under a full moon-lit sky, the proposal was made and accepted as Ed and Susan stood on the small bridge that crossed over a little man-made creek in the Bentley's backyard. At the requests of both sets of parents, the newly engaged couple agreed to get their degrees before getting married: Ed at Florida Southern and Susan with her degree in Elementary Education at Florida Atlantic University (FAU).

* * * * *

Upon Ed's return to FSC for his junior year, he was nominated and then elected to be the President of the Inter-Fraternity Council, the group that represented the eleven national fraternities on campus to the College President and its Board of Directors. While there were few issues that rose to the level of the College President's concern during his tenure, there was a monthly dialogue that was hosted by the College President and one or two members of the Board of Directors that Ed and other members of the Student Government organizations attended at one of the luxurious country clubs in the Lakeland area. The evenings were a monthly highlight for both the excellent presentation of food and because one his additional duties as the fraternities' representative required him to pick up the representative of the sororities on campus who just happened to be a former Miss Kentucky. It was tough duty but somebody had to do it.

* * * * *

By his junior year of college, it was clear that Ed felt the call to join the U.S. Army as a commissioned officer, and he worked hard to achieve that goal. In the summer between his junior and senior year, along with other fellow cadets who aspired to wear the gold bars of a Second Lieutenant, he went to the six weeks ROTC Summer Camp at Fort Bragg, North Carolina, adjacent to Fayetteville, North Carolina, in June and July 1968. The post, then as now, is the home of the Eighteenth Airborne Corps, the 82nd Airborne Division, and Special Forces.

After everyone in his platoon signed in, Ed found himself assigned as the Platoon Leader for his platoon, a position he held for the first three days of summer camp. During the latter part of his first week's training at Bragg, Susan's father, who had been suffering from lung cancer, died. The doctors attributed his death directly to smoking as he had been a heavy smoker his entire adult life. When the Platoon Tactical Officer (TAC), an infantry major, learned through the Red Cross what had happened, he gave Ed a five-day pass to go to the funeral. This was quite

12

an exception to policy since the cadet was not related to Susan's father, but the TAC authorized the pass anyway, showing great compassion for the situation.

Upon his return to Bragg after the funeral, Ed resumed training with his fellow cadets on basic squad and platoon tactics, weapons, field craft such as land navigation, physical fitness, negotiating through numerous obstacles courses, and drill and ceremonies. Sprinkled in the middle of this training was two days of kitchen police (KP) where DeVos learned the Army mess sergeant's techniques for peeling pounds of potatoes and cleaning the grease trap outside the mess hall. At the end of six weeks of training, this FSC student was tied with another cadet, a Citadel cadet, as the #1 cadet in their forty-man platoon, the highest standing of all the cadets from FSC. Based on this success and because it felt like the right thing to do, when it came time for him to fill out the form indicating his preferences as to which branch in the Army he would like to be assigned, Ed listed Infantry as his first choice. He never regretted that decision.

* * * * *

Because Susan had gone to college year around for three years and was on track to graduate from FAU in December, 1968 and would have her degree, and Ed would be commissioned on graduation day and would go immediately on active duty, she and Ed talked with his parents and her mother about them getting married in December 1968. After some discussion, permission was given, a date was set, and the two were married at Holy Spirit Roman Catholic Church in Lantana, Florida on 28 December 1968. This ceremony was in that church because Susan's background was Roman Catholic, and while Ed's had been Methodist, to ensure that they would be practicing the same faith, he began to attend the Catholic Church. Following the ceremony, they enjoyed their four-day honeymoon in Naples, Florida.

Once back from Naples, this newly-married couple packed their car and set off to Lakeland where they began their married life in a converted two-car garage apartment several blocks off campus for a rental fee of eighty-five dollars a month. Money was tight as they had a car and little else except for Ed's fifty dollar a month ROTC check, but with Susan's ability to be a substitute teacher in the Lakeland area, they made it through those days quite well, although both recall the night they ate at a Taco Bell restaurant using a fifty cent coupon from the college newspaper.

For some unknown reason, Ed made his best grades in college in his last semester and did that while he was still the Inter-Fraternity Council President as well as Cadet Battalion Commander of the college's ROTC program. Perhaps it was because he was no longer playing poker and/or bridge well into the wee hours of the morning at the fraternity house or going out to enjoy a mushroom pizza. Regardless, he was inducted into Omicron Delta Kappa, a leadership fraternity and ended up in the book of *Who's Who in Colleges and Universities for 1969*.

... Oh the memories. Those days helped form him and develop him. But now ... now it was time to look forward, not backward.

* * * * *

While Ed's growing up years provided a host of lessons learned, several stand out. First, each person must take responsibility for his actions. You can't blame someone else for something you did or didn't do. Tied to that is always do your best, and though there are no guarantees, rewards might come your way.

Second, keep focused on your goals. Just because you get knocked down by someone or from your own mistakes, doesn't mean you have to stay down. Get yourself up. Dust yourself off and get back to work.

Finally, Ed fumbled the ball badly as a young man. God touched his heart and he did not act on that. The young man in this story did not walk with God as he should have. But in God's graciousness, he did not give up on Ed. He was still guiding, leading, teaching, disciplining, and watching this young man, longing for the day when he would pay more attention to Him and His teachings. That day would come later, but the joy that Ed missed in his not having a very meaningful relationship with God was not God's fault. It was Ed's.

* * * * *

Lakeland still holds a place in the hearts of the DeVos', but not just because of their first days of marriage. Many years later, Ed's parents retired and moved from Florida to Lake Junaluska, North Carolina, about an hour or so from Western Carolina University where years later Kristen, Ed and Susan's daughter, would attend college. After living at Junaluska for almost twenty years, the elder DeVos' decided to move to a retirement community in Lakeland, Florida, appropriately enough called *The Carpenter's Home* where they both passed away to be with the Lord in 2000 and 2001.

2. FORT BENNING, GEORGIA. THE FIRST TIME

2LT Devos' orders stated that he would be at Fort Benning, Georgia for six months, from May to November 1969, during which time he would attend the U.S. Army's Airborne School, the Infantry Officer's Basic Course, and then Ranger School, the Army's premier small unit leader training course.

Fort Benning was named for Civil War Confederate General, Harry Benning, and was established in 1909 as Camp Benning. In 1920, Congress voted to make the post a permanent military installation and provided funds to officially designate it as the U.S. Army's Infantry School of Arms. In 1922, its name was changed from Camp Benning to Fort Benning and it encompassed a large land mass in parts of Georgia and Alabama and lies south of Columbus, Georgia. During the late 1960s, the topic which dominated the post was Vietnam. All the soldiers and their family members knew that every soldier was either going to Vietnam or had just gotten back from there and would probably be returning for another tour in the next twelve to eighteen months.

Showing up on this thirty-thousand man Army installation with its mix of buildings built in the 1920s and the newer construction, created quite a maze that this new 2LT had to negotiate as he attempted to sign in, but after a large run-around which tested both his patience and persistence, he accomplished his mission, and with it, came a big surprise. Because his orders stated that he would be going to Airborne School first, he was immediately entitled to jump pay of one hundred and ten dollars a month and the monthly 2LT's pay of three hundred and thirty dollars. In addition to those dollars, because his orders showed that his ultimate assignment was to be in Germany, he was also entitled to Temporary Duty Assignment (TDY) pay of four hundred dollars a month. Needless to say, when he reported all this to Susan later that night, they both realized they were in tall cotton—making eight hundred dollars a month, one month out of college. With that settled, they moved into one of the newer apartment complexes right off the traffic circle which led directly into Fort Benning's front gate three miles away.

* * * * *

In 1940, the Army established the Airborne School at Fort Benning with a test platoon of fifty men. Once the need for having paratroopers was fully recognized, the Army formed five divisions, the 11th Airborne, the 13th Airborne, the 17th Airborne, the 82nd Airborne, and the 101st Airborne, along with several separate parachute regiments and battalions in World War II. All these units were made up of volunteers and the training of those men in the World War II days had not changed much by the time DeVos began his paratrooper training in late May 1969.

The Airborne School instructors he was about to meet were professional in every respect. All were experienced paratroopers, each wearing silver Master Parachute wings indicating they were graduates of Jumpmaster school and each had more than sixty-five jumps, of which many were night jumps. Without exception, these men were all non-commissioned officers (NCOs), having served in airborne units such as the 82nd or 101st Airborne Divisions, and almost all of them wore a Combat Infantryman Badge (CIB) indicating they had seen ground combat as an infantryman, most of them in Vietnam. Some of the older instructors had a star over their CIB indicating they fought as infantrymen in two wars: Vietnam and in Korea in the early 1950s. These men were tough, hard-nose, physical specimens. They focused on making sure each potential paratrooper used all the proper parachute techniques that were taught, weeding out those who would be a danger to themselves or to others. Additionally, because these men had all served in airborne divisions, most of their jumps were "equipment jumps" as opposed to "Hollywood" jumps. These instructors were known as "Black Hats," for that was the distinctive headgear they wore. Only Airborne School instructors had earned the right to wear those black baseball caps with big airborne wings on them.

Regarding "equipment jumps" and "Hollywood jumps," the difference between the two was that on equipment jumps, the paratrooper was loaded down with his parachute, his rucksack full of gear fixed to his parachute harness below his reserve parachute and a weapons pouch filled with his weapon snapped to his parachute harness below his left arm and tied off further to his left leg. The weight the paratrooper carried on an equipment jump would be an additional fifty, sixty, seventy pounds, not counting his parachute. Hollywood jumps were made without the extra equipment.

With unbridled enthusiasm, DeVos started Ground Week, the first week of the three-week long course, with another five hundred hopefuls. To make a good impression, on who nobody knows, he began the first day of training wearing a brand new set of spit-shined jump boots, but because they were not sufficiently broken in, they were so stiff and unyielding to the lieutenant's feet, with all the running which amounted to eight miles each day, Ed found himself sidelined after two days because he couldn't walk, let alone run, because of the massive blisters on his feet.

After healing up, he started Ground Week again two weeks later, this time wearing some old worn-in boots.

Ground Week emphasized three fundamentals. Failure in any one of these three areas would result in being booted out of the course. The first point of emphasis was on being in top-notch physical shape which was tested daily through running and a lot of pull-ups. The second point of emphasis in this first week was to successfully make a correct PLF, short for parachute landing fall. This skill required a great amount of practice as you jumped from a platform that increased in height from two feet, to four feet, and then to six feet. The proper PLF required the paratrooper to roll after hitting the ground to spread the impact around the body instead of just on your feet. The last requirement of this first week was to make satisfactory exits from a simulated aircraft door from the thirty-four-foot tower with a parachute harness attached to a cable to get you safely to terra firma. Major signs of fear or panic from these practice exits from thirty-four feet up guaranteed an immediate release from the course by the ever-observant Black Hats.

Week Two was called Tower Week where the paratroopers continued to hone their skills from Ground Week and adding additional practice on PLFs from various heights and landings based on the wind conditions, all by using a device known as a swing landing trainer. Physical training requirements ramped up a bit, too, but by this second week of training, Ed and those with him were tougher and ready for more challenges. That came as each man was hauled two hundred and fifty up by a cable attached to the parachute hanging over his head. Once the paratrooper reached the top of the tower, the cable was released. Then the paratrooper had to steer his parachute in unpredictable winds and execute a proper PLF when he hit the ground. All in all, it was an exhilarating experience which increased the desire to jump from a real airplane twelve hundred feet above the ground. That came in Week Three.

With the weekend to contemplate what lay ahead, DeVos and the others with him started Week Three—Jump Week—where each man would make five jumps from an Air Force transport aircraft into a drop zone (DZ) located on the Alabama side of Fort Benning,. For at least half of the men Ed knew in his class, their first take-off from Lawson Army Airfield would be their first airplane ride. For those guys, they could honestly say they never landed in an airplane in their first five take-offs. For the record, Lawson Army Airfield is named in honor of two men named Lawson. The first man was a World War I pilot, Captain Walter R. Lawson who was killed in a crash in 1923. The second man, Captain Ted Lawson, author of the book, *Thirty Seconds Over Tokyo*, was one of the pilots on the Doolittle raid flown against Japan in 1942.

Waiting around to make that first jump on that Monday seemed to take forever. First, there were more PLFs to get the butterflies calmed down, then a long wait to draw the parachute you would be jumping, then more standing around until *finally*...the order was given to put your chute on. Then more inspections and then more waiting, the nervous chatter increasing minute by minute.

All of Ed's five jumps in Airborne School were made from a C-119 "Flying Boxcar," a Korean War vintage aircraft. The doors of the airplane were open even before take-off and since the flight time to the DZ from Lawson Army Airfield was only five minutes, as soon as the plane was off the ground, the Jumpmaster went through the time honored sequence of Jump Commands in thunderous shouts and hand signals. "Get Ready...Outboard Personnel Stand Up...Inboard Personnel Stand Up...Hook Up...Check Static Lines...Check Equipment...Sound Off For Equipment Check...Stand In the Door...Go". This sequence was always the same, and necessary, because of the noise from propellers, the air turbulence, and the need to insure the safety of every jumper, for once the green light came on at the door and the command to the first jumper was "Go," there was almost a stampede as the jumpers approached the open door ready to put their faith in their equipment, their training, and to test their courage.

Like the others with him, Ed followed instructions and stared at the horizon as he reached the door, not at the ground. Nevertheless, after he made that first leap of faith, he realized his first jump was a "night" jump; his eyes closed tight. But with a new confidence, he kept his eyes open on the second jump to get the whole experience: watching the airplane flying away from you, watching the parachute deploy as it flipped over his head. When he hit the ground on the DZ after his fifth jump three days later, the Black Hats pinned silver wings on his chest. 2nd Lieutenant Ed DeVos joined a special fraternity, a special breed of men with huge egos, declaring themselves to be lean, mean fighting machines. He was a United States Army Paratrooper. Airborne! No longer a dirty rotten leg—slang for "non-airborne qualified" personal.

* * * * *

Before moving on to the next two schools, now is a good time to add some details to a few of Ed's parachute jumps, as they overlap several assignments. As mentioned above, he went to Airborne School in May and early June 1969 and remained on Jump status while in Ranger School and through the fall of 1971 because he was assigned to the 509th Airborne Infantry in Mainz, Germany. In 1975-1976 Ed would again be on Jump status when he was assigned to be the Aide to the Commanding General (CG) at Fort Benning. It is important to note that while parachute jumping is statistically much safer than driving a car, things can happen to a paratrooper very quickly when he jumps out of a perfectly good airplane flying at one hundred and twenty miles an hour, one thousand feet above the ground, and Ed is living proof that things can (or almost can) happen. That is the case in four of his thirty-five jumps.

1

A night jump in Ranger School into Florida, November 1969. All the Ranger students were dead-tired from being awake the past forty-eight hours before they suited up to make this jump. This weariness contributed to the young lieutenant not tightening up the strap of his helmet before he exited the C-123. As soon as he left the aircraft, his helmet blew off his head, never to be seen again. This could have been disastrous because the DZ was bordered by some trees, and as you can image, the young officer, shall we say, was concerned because he could feel the wind blowing him in the direction of the tall pines as he drifted downward. With great effort, he was able to steer his parachute away from the trees before the wind had too much effect on his approach. The majority of those who jumped with him that night were not so fortunate.

2

A night jump into DZ Alzey southwest of the Rhine River in Germany with the 509th Airborne Infantry, early April 1970. This jump was out of a four-engine cargo jet, a C-141 Starlifter. For some unexplained reason, after this intrepid paratrooper exited the airplane, he realized instantly something was not right. There was no opening "shock" he had grown accustomed to as the parachute deployed and he could see the dark outlines of the other jumpers well above him, all signals that he had a malfunction, meaning his parachute had not properly deployed. Without hesitation he followed his training and pulled the handle to open his reserve parachute, watching it deploy immediately, and in what seemed like only five or ten seconds, he hit the ground, glad he had followed all the "What do you do if you have a malfunction" procedures that had been drilled into him and his fellow paratroopers by the Black Hats at

Fort Benning, who, over and over again, stressed that in situations like this, there is no time to think. Only time to react and execute the proper procedure. Later that night as this twenty-three year old soldier snuggled into bed next to Susan did he fully comprehend how serious the situation had been.

3

Another C-141 jump, this one on Exercise *Dawn Patrol I* near Aviano, Italy, close to the Italian Alps with the 509th Airborne Infantry in early June 1970. This was a mass tactical jump, nine C-141s flying in trail. All the paratroopers were making equipment jumps and DeVos had assigned himself the task of jumping with a heavy equipment bag which normally weighed another fifty pounds worth of radios in addition to the rest of his equipment. All totaled, this meant he would be jumping with one hundred and twenty pounds of additional equipment, not counting his parachute.

The heavy equipment bag is supposed to be released by the jumper when he is around one hundred feet off the ground and it is secured to the paratrooper's parachute with a long rope. Once the jumper releases the bag, it should drop thirty feet below the paratrooper and hit the ground "softly" so as not to damage the contents. But, when the lieutenant attempted to release the equipment bag, the ropes became tangled and he knew he would have to ride the bag in, regardless of all the weight he was carrying. Unable to even come close to making a proper PLF and after making a heavy thud on the Italian soil, Ed shook himself off and checked to see if the radios worked. Somehow they were no worse for wear despite the severe collision with the ground.

4

A helicopter jump at Fort Benning, Georgia, in the fall of 1975 when Ed was the Aide to the CG. On this day, this soldier was jumping a steerable parachute for the first time. This is a parachute much like the ones more experienced paratroopers use when they are making stand-up landings at the fifty-yard line at the big games like the Super Bowl. For this jump, Ed exited the UH-1 Huey at twenty-five hundred feet and was having a grand time making circles and twirls and spins until...he suddenly realized he was only fifty feet off the ground, and had not prepared himself mentally to land. With no reaction time left, this cocky paratrooper smashed in, hurting his back so severely, he was on physical therapy for several weeks, paying the price for his own negligence by not paying attention to the situation around him—a mistake for which he took responsibility.

* * * * *

Now, back to Fort Benning, June 1969. Our young warrior want-to-be went to the Infantry Officer Basic Course (IOBC) right after Airborne School. The purpose of this eight week course was for each newly commissioned Infantry officer to learn the skills, techniques, and leadership to lead a platoon of thirty-five to forty men into combat to accomplish the Infantry's primary mission: "To close with and destroy the enemy." Said another way, if all the Armed Forces were a long spear, the Infantry would be the point of the spear facing the enemy and destroying him in close combat while the rest of the spear behind the point all the way back to its end would provide the support the Infantry needed to accomplish its mission. The instructors at this school, like Airborne School, were experienced officers and NCOs. They knew their subjects, and without exception, they had served in Vietnam at least once and, in some cases, several tours. Each wore a CIB and the majority of these men were both Airborne and Ranger qualified. These were professional soldiers in every respect.

Because of the infantry's role in combat and with the high probability that each man in the class would be going to Vietnam at some point, the seriousness of the training in the field and in the classroom took on new meaning. The longer the class lasted, the attention paid to each instructor, regardless of the subject, increased. The variety of subjects covered a broad spectrum: leadership, marksmanship training using the M-16, the M-60 machine gun, and the M203 grenade launcher, day and night land navigation, communications and demolitions training, and all basic small unit infantry tactics, all with increased emphasis on physical fitness which was enhanced through obstacle courses, bayonet drills, hand-to-hand combat training, road marches, and long runs.

For Ed, IOBC was relatively easy due to the preparation he had received at FSC and then at Fort Bragg the previous summer, and with experience and the physical toughening up at Airborne School. While many of his classmates had received their commissions through one of the many ROTC programs taught at colleges across the United States, it was clear to him he had been well-prepared for these challenges. One of the highlights during this summer was for the DeVos' to go to one of Ed's friend's apartment, who was also a graduate of FSC, and watch America's first manned Lunar Landing on 20 July 1969.

After graduation from IOBC, DeVos had the good fortune of signing in early to Ranger School and since he was already Airborne qualified, he was assigned as an Assistant Instructor of Ranger Week for the Officer Candidate School (OCS) classes as they went out for their one week of a "Ranger" familiarization exercise. This gave him an excellent opportunity to observe Ranger Instructors (RIs) as they taught the OCS candidates practical Ranger field craft and patrolling teachings. He was also able to observe how the RIs would then grade these OCS candidates without the pressure of being a Ranger candidate himself. Another bonus was that Ed made his "cherry jump" out of a CH-47 Chinook helicopter with the RIs as they jumped into the exercise area. The term "cherry jump" refers to the first jump a paratrooper makes after Airborne School. It was quite educational as many units conduct their jumps a little differently from the schoolhouse, although the jump sequence in the aircraft described earlier never changes. Overall, this four-week period helped prepare him for the rigors he would face in Ranger School.

* * * * *

The history of the U.S. Army Rangers is long and filled with courage by those who served in these units. While the roots of the Rangers were planted in the Revolutionary War, most people think of World War II when Rangers scaled up the cliffs at Point Du Hoc at Normandy on D-Day, 6 June 1944. Six years later, in September 1950, Ranger training began in earnest after the outbreak of the Korean War with the training of seventeen Airborne Ranger companies. One year later, the Ranger Department was established at Fort Benning with the mission of providing Ranger qualified soldiers to all combat units.

2LT DeVos started Ranger School in late September and graduated just before Thanksgiving, 1969. He was in Class 5-70, nicknamed "Ranger Five. Eat 'em Alive." Since he would be "fully occupied" for nine weeks and would be unable to communicate with her except for only a few hours on two short breaks between phases, Susan went back to Florida to be with her family.

Ranger School is designed to push each soldier to his physical and mental limits for sixty-one days so the soldier will reach for his absolute full potential. Although Ed was physically in great shape like all the other volunteers, his weight dropped from one-hundred and eighty pounds

27

to one-fifty by graduation day; not unusual because Ranger students will eat an average twenty-two hundred calories a day, will carry sixty to ninety pounds of equipment over a total distances exceeding two hundred miles of tactical movements, getting between zero and five hours a sleep a night, and be physically challenged almost every waking hour.

Most of the Ranger candidates in Class 5-70 were in their early twenties, although a few were older; one man in DeVos' platoon was in his mid-thirties. This particular Ranger was a Special Forces NCO and while the men in this platoon helped cover for him on some of the physical challenges, his knowledge of field craft helped all of the men in the platoon later. There is no rank in Ranger School. You are just simply referred to as "Ranger _____" or by some other words that the RI would use to gain the soldier's absolute and full attention.

The instructors in Ranger School, not surprising, who were ever-present during Class 5-70's cycle, were all highly trained, highly motivated, professional NCOs, each man a combat veteran from Vietnam and each wore a Ranger Tab, Jump Wings, and a CIB. In Army vernacular, they were as tough as woodpecker lips. To receive a passing grade on patrols from any of these men required the Ranger candidate to really know his business, be able to demonstrate leadership in ever-changing situations, and be ready to adapt to accomplish the mission, regardless of what ever comes his way. No excuses — just results. As members of the 22nd Infantry Regiment would say, "Deeds not words."

To complete Ranger School and be awarded the coveted "Ranger Tab" is the goal of every Ranger candidate. To be awarded the Tab, you must show mastery of all the skills taught during the course, pass every physical challenge, of which there many, pass at least fifty per cent of a Go/No Go criteria when you are the designated patrol leader or assistant patrol leader, and to show a genuine willingness throughout the course to help your fellow Ranger candidates when they are in charge. The school is broken into three phases, each lasting just short of three weeks: The Fort Benning or "City" Phase, the Mountain Phase, and the Swamp Phase.

The Fort Benning Ranger camp is located in the southern section of the post and it starts with a water survival test which washed out about ten percent of those who started with DeVos as these men showed signs of fear of water. This is a safety issue because a great deal of Ranger training is around rivers, streams, and swamps, traversing through these areas at night. The training in this phase is heavy on small unit leadership, patrolling, and ambush tactics and techniques coupled with daily physical training challenges—long runs and road marches, obstacle courses like the "Darby Queen" which is similar to many of the "Ninja Warrior" obstacles currently seen on TV these days, and the "slide for life" and the "log walk" forty feet above the water. Integrated into this was weapons training, communications training, bayonet training, demolition training using C-4 to blow "stuff" up, hand-to-hand combat, and some difficult day and night land navigation challenges, to name just a few. For those who were Airborne qualified, these men made one jump during this phase. When Ed passed his first patrol with a solid "Go," it was a big relief and a confidence builder.

The Mountain phase is headquartered in Dahlonega, Georgia near the Appalachian Trail and Mount Yonah, one hundred and eighty-five miles north of Fort Benning. Because the patrols are conducted in mountainous terrain, the mastery of basic mountaineer skills is non-negotiable. These skills include day and night individual and buddy climbs, individual and rescue repels, and tying a number of rope knots that are used in mountaineer such as the bowline, prusik, and figure eight, to name just a few. The Ranger candidates then put all the knowledge from the Benning Phase and the Mountain Phase together as all patrols in this phase take place in the mountains. Class 5-70 went through this phase as the first snowfall of the winter fell, the crisp mountain air at night taking its toll on the already exhausted Rangers. Years later, Ed's nephew, 2LT Sean McElhenny, went through the mountain phase in December, a really cold, wet time. DeVos came out of this phase with another "Go" on his patrol, in good shape to get his Tab going into Florida.

The Florida phase is held in the swamps of the Yellow River at Eglin Air Force Base in the Florida Panhandle, two hundred and forty miles south of Fort Benning. Class 5-70 arrived there in early November. During this phase, everyone stayed constantly wet and cold because it seemed as though every patrol made at least one river crossing every night. Again, patrolling and setting up ambushes were the basic tactics employed as the class assaulted into the various operations by parachute, helicopter, or by RB 15s (rubber rafts) from a Navy landing craft out in the Gulf of Mexico. During this phase, instructors gave the men some survival training regarding the local poisonous and non-poisonous snakes and on booby traps employed by the North Vietnamese Army (NVA) and Viet Cong (VC) in Vietnam. This phase is designed to test every member of the class to his maximum capability. Patrols were longer and more difficult, partly because everyone was hurting, tired, hungry, and physically worn down. Many in the class, including Ed, had exposure or minor frostbite in their hands and/or feet, but since this was the last phase, the driving thought in everyone's mind was to put one foot in front of the other and convince yourself to hang in there. The basic attitude was, "I've come too far to quit now."

During this phase, DeVos got a "No Go" on one of his patrols as his failure to pay attention cost him. Nevertheless, he knew if he could gut it out to the end—no small feat—he would get the Tab. Like most of the men who were "good" on patrols, Ed and the others in that category carried the radios or the machine guns so the guys who needed to pass their patrols would be as rested and alert as possible. In Ranger School, this is known as "cooperate and graduate."

There were some men who held on all the way to the end but did not graduate with the Tab. In Ranger School each man has a "Ranger Buddy," a fellow Ranger who is there to encourage you and help you. This man will be by your side when you are hurting; he may look for ticks on your body just as you look for ticks on his. He may help pop your blisters just as you pop his. Ed's first "Ranger Buddy" got hurt in the mountains and so he was assigned another man, one whose buddy had become sidelined. This second "Ranger Buddy" was an Engineer officer, so many of the skills needed in Ranger School were new to this man. While this man mastered the necessary requirements needed, he was generally uncooperative when tasked by another Ranger to carry the radio or the machine gun. Over time, this began to cause problems because this individual did not understand the meaning behind "cooperate and graduate."

In the Swamp Phase, this man's attitude caught up with him as he failed the "Peer Evaluation" at the end of that phase. This is an evaluation that is held in each platoon at the end of each phase to weed out those Ranger Candidates who care more about themselves than they do about the team and its mission. While this man finished the course, he was not awarded a Tab. Nine weeks down the drain because he put himself ahead of others.

Ranger stories can last and last, and for the most part, almost all of them are true. Embellished a bit, perhaps, but true, nevertheless. So, rather than spend time here in relating a tale or two, some stories are for another time and another place. Their full and complete description will require a bit of modest libation.

Our young warrior in this story, now twenty-two years old, finished Ranger School two days before Thanksgiving. After turning in their equipment, he and another Ranger drove to Atlanta to catch a flight to West Palm Beach. While both of these men wore their green dress uniforms, for some strange reason both of them were "carded" at the Atlanta Airport as they tried to get a beer. Perhaps it was because they were both skin and bones and had this far-away "I'm beat" look that caused the bartender to check IDs.

Once home, the effects of the last few months took hold as DeVos' system rebelled against turkey and all the fixings. It was rather embarrassing, but later that night food went down a little easier the second time. That did not stop this newly minted Ranger from falling asleep on the bathroom toilet later that night. It was also difficult to have sheets touch his toes as his feet were so raw that even the mere touch of the cloth stung them.

Like all those who have gone through this experience and been awarded the Ranger Tab, this soldier is always proud to say, "Rangers Lead the Way." Of the three hundred and twenty highly motivated volunteers that started Ranger Class 5-70, less than one hundred and fifty graduated with the Ranger Tab. These pass/fail rates were common, and they testify as to how difficult Ranger School is and that even very motivated people can fail or get hurt along the way. Since those days, Ed has known several men who failed to get the Ranger Tab the first time, yet they went back again years later and got the Tab. They have his utmost respect.

After returning to Fort Benning with Susan for some final out-processing, final preparations began for the move to Germany. When a moving van arrived at Susan's home to pick up their household goods, the five boxes the two men loaded on their truck took about fifteen minutes.

* * * * *

The lessons this young lieutenant learned during those months at Fort Benning could fill many pages: fundamentals of the trade that would help him lead men, accomplish his mission, and survive. Every day provided new information or ways to improve on the basics he was already familiar with. But, without question, the major lessons he took with him had to do with the mind.

Those days and nights in Airborne and Ranger Schools taught him you can do more than you think you can. You can always take one more step. You can always pull yourself up higher if you think you can. Just keep giving it your best every day. Understand that you can improve your best. For example, let's say today you can only do fifty pushups at one time, but, if you keep doing those fifty pushups every day, soon you will be able to do fifty-five, or sixty, or seventy. If you work at getting better at some skill you desire to master, you can achieve it if you put in the appropriate effort and time. The bigger the goal you have, the more time, effort, and energy it will take to achieve it.

A second point. Say what you mean and mean what you say. Be a person that can be counted on because your word is your bond. In the Infantry, all those around you are depending on your word being your bond. They trust every word you speak just as you should be able to trust every word they speak. Each man is depending on the other. Always mean what you say and say what you mean. Be a person others can trust because they know you will do what you said you would do.

Finally, develop "situational awareness." Tune all of your senses to always be on alert. Smells, sounds, what you see, and what you feel in your gut will tell you when something is or is not right. Learn to trust your senses. Be aware of your surroundings. Be aware of what those around you are telling you and what they are not telling you. Study the reactions of faces and body language. Their words may say one thing, but their body language may tell a different story. Once you become a good student of "reading" others, you will begin to recognize when others need help, or a hand up, or some encouragement. Then use your best judgment. Don't ignore the problem. Trust your instinct and do something. As my wise daughter, Kristen tells her daughter, "Do the right thing."

3. 509TH AIRBORNE INFANTRY. MAINZ GERMANY. A PERIOD OF MATURING

In early January 1970, Lieutenant DeVos flew from West Palm Beach to Charleston, South Carolina, where he then boarded a direct flight to Rhein-Main Air Base, which is adjacent to the Frankfurt International Airport in West Germany. This was a contract flight filled with servicemen and women, some with families, some without, all assigned to various units throughout Europe. Because there were no quarters available for the DeVos,' Susan would fly over at a later time once her husband had secured U.S. government housing. This was expected to take about thirty days.

His orders assigned him to the 2nd Battalion of the 509th Airborne/Mechanized Infantry, one of two infantry battalions stationed in Lee Barracks, Mainz-Gonsenheim, part of the 1st Brigade (Airborne) of the 8th Infantry Division (Mechanized). To be assigned to this unit was an honor as the history of the 509th Airborne Infantry is well-known in airborne circles as it was the first U.S. unit to make a combat parachute assault in World War II, flying fifteen hundred miles from England to jump into North Africa in *Operation Torch* in November, 1942. The 509th then fought with distinction at other locations during the remainder of the war: Italy, Southern France, and in the Battle of the Bulge. The colors red, white, and blue are dominate on the crest and a paratrooper occupies a prominent place at its top middle of the crest while the slogan of the regiment, "All the Way," is at the bottom.

Mainz was founded by the Romans in the 1st Century B.C. and was the home of Joseph Gutenburg who invented the first moveable type-printing press in 1440. In 1450, he began to produce books including what became known as the Gutenburg Bible. During World War II, the city suffered from Allied bombers but in 1970 there was little evidence remaining of those air attacks. The city is forty kilometers southwest of Frankfurt and sits across the Rhine River from Wiesbaden, at that time the Headquarters for the U.S. Air Force Europe. Mainz, a city in those days of around 100,000 citizens is now double that size. The smaller Main River intersects the Rhine near the city's center.

After landing at Rhein-Main, DeVos was met by another officer from the 2-509 who informed him that the 1st Brigade was in the field near the Czechoslovakian border at Grafenwoehr (Graf), a large training area the German Army used in both World War I and II which had been taken over by the U.S. Army at the war's end. It was now a major training site for our Army with enough maneuver area to conduct major exercises as well as to shoot all our weapons to prepare for any eventuality, including defense of Western Europe against any Russian advances; the primary threat to U.S. forces in Germany and the other armed forces from the Allied and NATO countries in the European Theater. Anxious to go to work, once this 2LT dropped his bags at the Bachelor Officer's Quarters (BOQ) and drew his equipment from the supply area, he climbed aboard a two and one-half ton truck, called a deuce and a half, at dusk and tried to catch up on his sleep during the six-hour ride to Graf.

* * * * *

The Eastern Bavaria region of Germany in early January is always cold with several feet of snow lining the roads. In January 1970, the weather conditions were normal. When the deuce and a half worked its way into the backwoods of the training area just before dawn the next day, the others on the vehicle along with the lieutenant tumbled out. They had arrived at their destination: the Command Post (CP) of the 2nd Battalion, 509th Airborne Mechanized Infantry. It was a small group of three tents surrounded by a number of radio antennas. Soldiers moved about the area with a purpose; an expectation that something was about to happen filled the air.

Once he received some directions, DeVos, three months short of his twenty-third birthday, met Lieutenant Colonel (LTC) Ted Jenes, a man who years later would retire with the rank of Lieutenant General. A soft-spoken officer, he didn't mince words that brisk morning. He looked at the lieutenant and noted his jump wings and his Ranger Tab on his uniform before he spoke, his sleepy eyes showing the strain of the past few days, saying something to the effect of, "Welcome to the battalion, Lieutenant. Glad you're here. We are short of officers so I'm assigning you to be our Recon Platoon Leader. SFC Mathews, your Platoon Sergeant, will brief you on what we've got going. As you may have heard, we're about to begin the battalion's ORTT (Operational Readiness Training Test) so you've got about thirty minutes to link up with your platoon before you cross the LD. I'll talk to you later. Don't have time right now. Glad you're here. Airborne."

The translation of the above conversation is that LTC Jenes had been up most of the night getting ready for the battalion's ORTT, a major event for the unit. Because he had spent the last day or two planning, issuing orders, and checking on a number of things before the battalion would begin this test when it crossed the Line of Departure (LD), the battalion commander didn't have time to talk. Because the battalion was short of officers, he was forced to put this brand new, who-knows-from-where, lieutenant in charge of one of the most important platoons in the battalion because that platoon is the "eyes and ears" of the battalion as it deploys in front of the unit to "find the enemy" to "develop the situation." The Platoon Sergeant, Sergeant First Class (SFC) Mathews would give this new guy the details on this mission and he would be watching this new LT like a hawk to make sure the platoon accomplished its mission. Now, Lieutenant, get out of here. Go find your platoon, and implied in all this was the over-riding thought, "Don't screw it up."

With LTC Jenes' words ringing through his head, this brand new to the unit, wet behind the ears, butter bar 2nd Lieutenant, got directions to the Recon Platoon which was just over the next hill. SFC Mathews, a grizzled thirty-four-year old veteran of two tours in Vietnam, a CIB and jump wings on his uniform, greeted DeVos as he stumbled into the platoon area. After a quick salute, the Platoon Sergeant took about five minutes to brief his new Platoon Leader on the plan as they looked at a map pushed up against the side of one of the ten M-114s, a tracked reconnaissance vehicle, that belonged to the platoon.

As he finished briefing the officer, SFC Mathews pointed, "We should be headin' out in that direction in about ten minutes to cross the LD on time." As the lieutenant absorbed all he had been told and after studying the map again for the second or third time, he looked at his Platoon Sergeant and said, "Sergeant Mathews, I heard what you said but it looks to me we should be going in that direction over there," pointing to a small hill ninety degrees away from the direction SFC Mathews had indicated. The sergeant looked at the lieutenant a second time and then smiled. "You know, Lieutenant, I believe you're right. Good call." Turning around, he smiled at the other NCOs nearby and gave them a "thumbs up" as he announced, "You heard the LT. Mount up."

It had been a subtle test and the new Platoon Leader had passed. From that moment on, SFC Mathews spent all the time necessary to help the wet-behind the ears officer become the best platoon leader possible. In the years that followed, Ed wondered many times what direction his Army career would have taken if he had failed SFC Mathews' test.

* * * * *

After the highly successful ORTT for the battalion was in the books, and the focus turned toward other training at Graf, all the lieutenants in the battalion slept in a large Quonset hut on the edge of the cantonment area. It was great to begin bonding with these men DeVos would serve with, in some cases, for many years to come. It was a mix of ROTC and West Point commissioned officers, all Airborne qualified and most had their Ranger Tab as well. Although that was fifty years ago, these officers who are still living remain friends today, as do their wives because of the shared experiences in this battalion. Names like Male, Skull, Caprio, Griffith, Sullivan, Watson, Thorstens, Snow, McCrary, Clukey, and Mitchell are among those the DeVos' share Christmas cards with. Over the years this group has held reunions in places such as Denver, Atlanta, Fort Benning, Washington D.C., Atlanta, Boston, and Lexington, KY. Most interesting is that the vast majority of these men served their country for over twenty years, commanding battalions and serving as senior staff officers in many higher headquarters to include the Pentagon. To a man, they express the view that they stayed in the Army for all those years because of what they learned, felt, saw, and experienced in their time in 2-509 Airborne Infantry, a great tribute to the senior leadership team in this unit.

When reunions are held and as old stories are told and then retold, one of the tales that gets special attention has to do with the Lieutenant's Quonset hut at Graf. In the middle of the cold nights when the snow was piling up and these young men felt the call of nature, it was expected that they should don enough clothes to use the latrine one hundred yards away, regardless of the depth of the snow. A second option—the quicker one by far—was to simply make a mad dash outside this metal building and do your business in the snow. Since this second option was preferable at 0200 on any given night, there was clear evidence in the snow in the light of day the next morning of what had transpired.

The Brigade Commander, we will call him "Colonel Smith," decreed one day that he did not wish to see any more yellow stains in the snow piles outside the officer's quarters as he expected all these officers to be gentlemen and walk to the distant latrine in their moment of need, regardless of how cold it was. Not surprising, the day after his declaration, there was an even greater amount of evidence that showed that many disregarded his wishes, but since there was no way to find out who the culprit (s) was/were, all the officers got a lecture from COL Smith, and to his credit, that was the end of the matter. To the lieutenants the lesson learned was—Never give an order that you can't enforce. It makes you look like a fool.

* * * * *

Once the battalion left Graf and got back to Mainz, it was time to observe some real leaders at work. Besides LTC Jenes, 2-509 Airborne Infantry was blessed with two other men who made up the senior leadership team of the battalion: Major C.Q. Williams, nicknamed "Smoke," and Command Sergeant Major (CSM) Bill Edge. Major Williams was the second man to earn the Medal of Honor in Vietnam. To know of his exploits in battle as a 2nd Lieutenant caused everyone to hang on his every word. He didn't have to say too much to have his requests followed instantly. CSM Edge, one of the original members of the U.S. Army's Parachute Team founded in 1959, called the *Golden Knights*, was a bit quieter but he exhibited leadership with every step he took and with every penetrating glance he gave. His look was, at times, worth ten thousand words. He was always teaching those young officers he felt had potential and DeVos was fortunate enough to be one of those he counseled on numerous occasions. When he retired, CSM Edge had made over seven thousand parachute jumps and was the Command Sergeant Major of Special Forces. Both of these men have passed away, but their influence still lives in many today.

During these first few days back in Mainz, Ed was able to get temporary quarters so Susan could join him. He also got his international driver's license. On the day Susan was to arrive, her husband found himself on a rifle range that required his presence, and through a series of mishaps, he borrowed another officer's car to make the mad dash to Rhein Main, running about an hour later than he intended. Totally inexcusable! And wouldn't you know it, Susan's plane was on time instead of being the typical two or three hours late.

Fortunately, one of the couples that flew over with her kept her company until the young officer could be seen running through the airport to find his wife. To put the icing on the cake, as they started the drive back to Mainz, it started to snow quite heavily. This would not have been too difficult except that the windshield wipers of this borrowed car did not operate properly which required both the driver and his passenger to put their hands out the windows to brush the snow off the windshield as they drove along the busy autobahn. Since this was Susan's first experience with snow, it was a day to remember. What saved the day for DeVos was that he had been smart enough to reserve a room in the Mainz Hilton for three nights which had a magnificent view of the Rhine River.

A few days later, they moved into temporary quarters on the fourth floor of one building for about four weeks before securing permanent quarters near the Officers Club in an area called Mainz University Housing Area (MUHA), this one on the first floor, next to the fence on a main street where a beer and bratwurst stand was located. They also bought a brand-new Volkswagen Beetle for sixteen hundred dollars right off the German showroom floor.

Susan bonded immediately with the other lieutenant's wives — Marlene, Michee, Skip, Sue, Sarah Kay, Maxine, and others. These women stayed close to each other, comforting one another as their husbands were in the field, organizing parties, taking walks together to see the historical points of interest in Mainz, learning to speak German with some real Southern accents, helping each other as babies were born, visiting quaint nearby German villages, and in general, keepings tabs on one another, knowing that sooner or later, their husbands were going to receive orders for Vietnam.

They formed an invaluable sisterhood that few outside the Armed Forces could ever understand. They raised their families and kept the households running, all while putting on a show of great strength as they worried about the men they loved, all of whom lived by the motto "Danger is no stranger to an Airborne Ranger."

* * * * *

The next fifteen months went by quickly as this unit faced one challenge after another. There were constant deployments back to Graf or to other training areas like Baumholder and the Taunus Mountains. There were jumps into Vilseck, Finthen, Alzey, with the German Airborne at Altenstadt, or Bad Kreuznach, where DeVos and some others made five helicopter jumps in one day, all with German jumpmasters, and there was the jump into Italy which was mentioned in the previous chapter. All of the lieutenants had a multitude of additional duties that took them away from training, like supervising the guards at the Budenheim ammunition dump, staying in the battalion area as the battalion staff duty officer at night, or settling claims against the U.S. government made by German farmers who had their farm equipment damaged when they ran over some paratrooper's gear left behind after one of the unit's jumps.

Weekend social events, monthly battalion hail and farewells on Rhine River cruises, visiting the Christmas markets, taking weekend leave to see the Louvre Museum and the Folies Bergere in Paris, windmills and colorful tulips at springtime in Holland, the German Alps at Hitler's Eagle's Nest near Berchtesgaden in the cold of February, coupled with many spontaneous gatherings around MUHA, helped ease the tension of the days.

Putting a real drain on training was the battalion's dual mission—one Mechanized and one Airborne. With the mix of M-113s, M-114s, and M-578s mechanized vehicles, to name a few, all of which would be needed to fight the Russians hordes should they attack, much of the battalion's time was invested in keeping these tracked vehicles in proper mechanical condition. Because the prerequisite to be in this airborne unit was to be a paratrooper, few of its officers, NCOs, or soldiers had much experience maintaining these vehicles, let alone how to fight from them.

The truth be told, the battalion spent much more time maintaining proficiency to accomplish its Airborne mission; the ability to rapidly project U.S. presence in this part of the world. This not only required that all members of the unit make periodic jumps to keep up their skill, it also meant the battalion had a second set of vehicles that could be dropped by parachute, thereby doubling the maintenance issues for the entire unit. During the time Ed was in 2-509, there were two occasions that warranted serious planning to possibly jump into another country to protect U.S. citizens. Neither of those situations got to the boiling point, but those times, along with keeping a watchful eye on all the space launches out of Cape Kennedy, caused the unit to remain in a high state of vigilance. With the knowledge that contingencies can occur without much warning, the Airborne mission drove the train and the concern about the mechanized vehicles took a back seat.

In addition to the real-world possibilities, there was the normal training of weapons, communications, Expert Infantryman's Badge (EIB) testing, gas warfare, tactics, and daily physical training. During one bridging exercise, elements of the battalion crossed the Rhine River at the same spot where the 5th Infantry Division, part of Patton's Third Army, crossed in 1945.

Because the unit was always undermanned due to personal requirements in Vietnam, one of Ed's jobs as the Recon Platoon Leader was to travel to Rhein Main Air Force Base once a week to give a short talk to soldiers arriving in Germany to try and convince them to volunteer to join this elite Airborne unit.

This effort was moderately successful and those soldiers who volunteered had their orders changed and were immediately diverted to the First Brigade (Airborne). These men soon found themselves going through the brigade's Jump School at Wiesbaden Air Force Base, a mirror image of Fort Benning's as this school was run by NCOs who previously had served as instructors there. While other units in Germany were not happy about the loss of their inbound replacements, the "recruiting" effort was blessed by Headquarters Europe, so there wasn't much they could say about it.

In another bit of good fortune, DeVos was selected to attend the five-day Air-Ground Operations School (AGOS) at Ramstein Air Force Base in Kaiserslautern, an hour's drive south of Mainz. It was a good break as Susan went with him. Much of what he learned at this school came in handy during some of the tougher days in Vietnam two years later.

* * * * *

No discussion of the 2-509 Airborne Infantry would be complete if the story about the Silver Bullet Award was omitted. While there are many versions of this yarn, only three men were present when this incident took place: DeVos and two others, "Joe" and "Pete."

In 1970, the Army paid its soldiers in cash each month. To do so, each company detailed two of its officers to make the proper payments to all its soldiers. One payday morning, Joe and Ed reported to the NCO Club at Lee Barracks at 0330. Each was armed with a .45 caliber pistol. After receiving the cash the Finance Office deemed was the correct amount for the company, these two officers counted and recounted the amount to make sure they agreed with the Finance's numbers. They then signed the appropriate papers, left the NCO Club, and walked back to the unit area.

Upon arrival at the company, per SOP, they counted out the dollars per the pay sheet that each soldier was entitled to. Those dollars were then put into an envelope with each soldier's name on it. Once each man reported to these two officers, the officers would then count out the money each soldier was to receive and witness his signature, attesting to the fact that the soldier received the pay due him per the Finance Office.

All the money was accounted for and Joe and Ed were ready to begin the actual payment to the soldiers who were now lined up outside the small office they occupied. The door to the office was closed. During the counting process, Pete had come into the office since this was the "hang out" room for the lieutenants. Since Ed had missed the .45 class at Fort Benning or because he had been asleep that day, he made some off-the-wall comment along the lines of, "Don't know why we've got these .45s. Don't even remember how to use it."

Joe was nearest and volunteered, "I'll show you." With that he pulled out his weapon and BLAM. The round pinged around the small room, somehow missing all three of the young officers. Shakily, Ed said, "Joe, put that down!" Joe responded, "OK. Let me make sure it's clear." Another BLAM. This round went straight into the desk in front of the three men. All those soldiers waiting outside the room in the pay line were real quiet. Finally, somebody asked through the closed door, "Are you guys OK in there?" to which the three officers responded. "Yeah, we're OK."

Before the officers opened the door to begin paying the soldiers, they found both bullets. The first one was a splattered mess from hitting all the walls of the room. The second bullet—the one in the desk—was in good shape. No scars. No dents. Nothing.

Later, after the three highly embarrassed young men were appropriately dressed down, that second bullet—*The Silver Bullet*—was then presented at each monthly battalion "Hail and Farewell" to the officer who screwed up the most during the previous month. That officer was to keep this bullet with him at all times, maintaining it in a highly polished state. If he did not have the bullet with him or if it was not highly polished, he would be buying drinks for one and all. Everything was fine with the award for about the next six months until the new battalion commander, we will call him "LTC Brown," was nominated to receive the coveted award because of some big screw-up on his part. Needless to say, LTC Brown failed to see the humor of that presentation and the *Silver Bullet Award* ceased to exist from that time forward. For safe keeping, this bullet is now in the hands of one of the officers who was involved in this story; a reminder of that day, that unit, and of the good men who served in it.

* * * * *

Sadly, DeVos' time in the Recon Platoon lasted only three months because with the shuttle of officers coming and going to Vietnam, he became the Support Platoon Leader, responsible for the beans and bullets for the battalion—a thankless but important task. Like with the Recon Platoon, his Platoon Sergeant, SFC Long, was squared away and they worked well together. Just when things were running smoothly, the Battalion S-4, the battalion's logistics officer, got orders for Vietnam so Ed found himself doing both jobs — a captain's job (S-4) and the Support Platoon Leader's job (1st Lieutenant) all while he was a 2LT. He was blessed again with another sharp NCO, SFC Funderberk, the battalion's Mess Sergeant who kept the soldiers well fed both in the field and in garrison. Since another additional duty Ed now had was to be the Battalion Mess Officer, having a man like SFC Funderberk around saved this officer's "bacon" more than once. It was clear from his girth, SFC Funerberk was not only an excellent cook but he made it a point to conduct a quality control check on everything his mess hall prepared.

After the Italy jump, two events occurred worth noting. First, all the 2nd Lieutenants with a date of rank of 4 June 1969 were promoted to 1st Lieutenant on 4 June 1970. In looking back at those days, those promoted that day were not much smarter than when they joined the battalion but they were a bit wiser; more experienced, more understanding about soldiers and NCOs, each developing a sixth sense so critical when dealing with others. Second, since all good things must come to an end, LTC Jenes' command of the battalion ended as he was moved up to Headquarters, 8th Infantry Division to become the G-3, the operations officer of the division, a job that clearly pointed toward further advancement. His replacement, the aforementioned "LTC Brown," came from West Point where he had been an instructor in the Physical Fitness Department for several years. While the officers in the battalion knew LTC Jenes to be a man of substance and character, a man one would do well to emulate, he was a hard act to follow. LTC Brown seemed more interested in style. His priorities were never articulated in ways easily understood, but the officers and NCOs soldered on, continuing to give their best even if the direction of the unit was not well defined.

With this change of battalion commanders, 1LT DeVos had a new position. He became the Battalion's S-1: the personnel/administrative officer for the unit. A major part of this job was to keep all the admin in the unit flowing correctly and efficiently, both internally and to and from higher headquarters. Because LTC Brown was a consummate nitpicker, particularly when it came to paper, Ed was constantly tested on the vast amount of papers that flowed to and from his office. His savior in those days was CSM Edge as he kept this officer grounded, giving him pointers on how to negotiate the mine fields of supervising the daily grind of all the battalion administration.

The one highlight that came Ed's way occurred when he was buried in papers one night preparing for a big inspection from the Division Inspector General's (IG) office. In the back of an old file cabinet, he found an original copy of the After Action Report (AAR) of the 2-509 Airborne Infantry's World War II jump into North Africa. Before informing LTC Brown about this find, the lieutenant read through the lengthy report, discovering that the problems those men faced in 1942 were the same problems that continued to plague the unit now: how to assemble the unit after making a night jump. While the airplanes had changed—from C-47s in World War II to C-130s and C-141s, the fog of war and the uncertainty of the situation in an airborne drop remained the same. A valuable discovery.

After surviving six months as S-1, as other shortages occurred, Ed became the assistant S-3 of the battalion and then almost without warning, he found himself sitting in the S-3's chair, a Major's slot. This proved to be another significant learning experience when the battalion deployed to Baumholder and exercised against other units. It was another time where this officer was held up tall by two stalwart NCOs, SFC Freeze and SFC Schrader. They kept this man on the straight and narrow path of success and made him look far better than what he was.

* * * * *

After returning from Baumholder, Ed took Susan out for her twenty-fourth birthday to a wonderful Hungarian restaurant downtown and the next morning he was passing out cigars celebrating the birth of a baby girl named Kristen Kay DeVos, who was born in the Air Force hospital across the river in Wiesbaden. As this family of three grew together, the rookie father, after much practice, finally learned how to change the diapers of this defenseless little girl without sticking her with the sharp end of a pin. Then there was the night when he was rocking this little one to sleep in the rocking chair in her bedroom when he fell asleep before she did. Obviously, he had a lot to learn about fatherhood, but he was willing to keep trying and Susan was a great teacher. As time approached for this threesome to depart Germany, one of the "must-do's" was to take the proper documents to the American Embassy in Frankfurt to get this little girl her U.S. citizenship paperwork. Soon after this, Ed was promoted to Captain on 4 June 1971, two years after his commissioning.

The family left Mainz in August 1971 with Ed's orders in hand to attend a six-week temporary duty assignment (TDY) at the Military Assistance Training for Advisors (MATA) Course at Fort Bragg, North Carolina before he left for Vietnam.

$$* * * * *$$

Those days in the 509th provided a host of lessons learned that were not forgotten. One of the most valuable is that you can always do more than you think you can. The pace of the unit required the officers to grow up fast, to be responsible to perform duties well above what would normally be expected of their rank and level of experience. Mistakes were made, but with each mistake came growth. As one very senior officer stated, "If you could survive the 509th in those days, you will be a success wherever you will be assigned later."

A second great lesson was trust your NCOs. The smart officer will lean on the NCOs. These professionals had seen it before and if you listened to them and asked them for their thoughts, their opinions, and their ideas, they were never shy about sharing them. While what they might suggest or recommend may or may not fit the particular question or situation, their thoughts broadened the young officer's options and thinking. Another plus, when a bond is formed with your NCOs, your team is much stronger.

A third piece of advice came from Ted Jenes who taught his new lieutenants his three rules to success: "Have patience, be flexible, and have a sense of humor (be able to laugh at yourself)." Over the years, Ed added one more rule to those three: "Keep your perspective."

Finally, when there was time to think and study more about war, it became clear to DeVos that whether you go to battle in a tracked vehicle, by parachute, or by helicopter, once you hit the ground, the real battle, the real reason for driving or jumping or flying into battle, all comes down to the last one hundred yards to the objective. Us against them. All the time and preparation to ride, jump, or fly into battle doesn't mean a thing if our soldiers are not prepared to win in the last one hundred yards. The riding, jumping, and flying were just the means of transportation to get you to that piece of ground where the real work begins.

4. VIETNAM. THE "QUIET" TIME

When Captain and Mrs. DeVos arrived at Fort Bragg, North Carolina in mid-September 1971, they knew the situation. They would be there for eight weeks as Ed went through the Military Assistance Training for Advisors (MATA) Course, and then he would fly to Vietnam and be assigned to a Vietnamese organization somewhere in South Vietnam. The purpose of the MATA Course was to learn as much of the Vietnamese language and culture that the Vietnamese instructors could cram into their students so that these advisors-to-be could have a meaningful relationship with the Vietnamese soldiers and officials they would be assigned to assist. The language classes gave each student a base to start learning more of the language before they arrived in Vietnam. The course did not address any war fighting skills or tactics since most of those who were in this class would be stationed in provincial cities or towns. Because the drawdown of U. S. military involvement in Vietnam was now in full swing, few would be with Vietnamese combat units.

Based on this, the couple rented a small apartment three miles south of the main gate of Fort Bragg and spent as much time together as they could with their daughter, Kristen, now five months old, in the center of it all. The most frightening event that happened to the family occurred one evening when Kristen somehow managed to pull a small portable TV down from a table, putting a deep gash around her nose, thereby prompting a quick trip on post to Womack Army Hospital. Within a short time, as her father watched with a careful eye, a young doctor stitched up the wound as Kristen cried the whole time, her father feeling every poke of the needle as his little girl looked up at him. As this man was just about finished with the stitches, he stepped back for a moment to examine his work. After further examination, the doctor said that he was afraid that the stitches he had just put in would leave a scar and so he wanted Ed's permission to take those stitches out and be more careful on his second try. Reluctantly, the captain agreed and to this day, he is still grateful he made that decision as Kristen shows no evidence of this early trauma to her face.

As soon as the MATA Course was over, the family drove back to their home town of Lake Worth, Florida and purchased a small two bedroom home a mile from both Susan's mother and Ed's parents. While neither of them voiced it, Ed could breathe easier knowing that Susan would be near loved ones. After he deployed, Susan's twin sister, Katherine, moved in with her. A plus for all concerned.

It was during this time at Fort Bragg that Ed began to have a better appreciation for what military wives go through. Their husbands go to war with no guarantee of their return. The same can be said for every time the soldier walked out the door to perform his duties such as making a parachute jump, fly his jet or helicopter, setting demolitions to blow "stuff" up, or execute some other inherently dangerous task. This was something Susan lived with every day of their marriage and she was just one of many who experienced this. Even during their time at Bragg, Ed realized that she was lonely, away from family and friends, and fearful of the unknowns. If something happened to him and he did not return from Vietnam, the burden of caring for their daughter rested solely on her. As these thoughts whirled around in his head, he realized the best chance for him to get home safely rested on his ability to do the best job possible. However, the enormity of the possibilities weighed heavy from time-to-time.

* * * * *

On 6 December 1971, the twenty-four year old captain flew to Oakland, California and then boarded a contract airliner with two hundred other soldiers and airmen whose final destination was Tan Son Nhut Airfield in Saigon, the capital city of South Vietnam, a city of over a million people sitting astride the Saigon River. After the war ended in 1975, the name of the city was changed to Ho Chi Minh City and today, it is the home of more than eight million people. On that flight in 1971, there was a two-hour stop in Manila in the Philippines before the 707 spiraled down from a high altitude to avoid enemy gunfire before landing early the next morning at Tan Son Nhut.

As the doors of the plane opened, a foul, distinct smell filled the lungs of each passenger as he stepped out, an experience that was and still is, common in most third world countries because of the combination of sweltering heat, high humidity, and unsanitary conditions. Regardless, everyone was hustled from the plane into a one story terminal building to several desks where admin personnel checked each man's orders. Since DeVos was assigned to Military Assistance Command, Vietnam (MACV), he and others who were to be in that command boarded a rickety military bus and were taken several miles away to another set of buildings where they received a short briefing and another check of orders. Then it was time to get some rest and food with instructions to report back the next morning. With more questions than answers, that was day one in Vietnam.

The next two days passed in a blur as the captain was told he would be assigned to Team 51, the team of U.S. advisors with the 21st Division of the Army of South Vietnam (21st ARVN), part of Military Region 4 (MR-4), one of four areas South Vietnam was divided into: MR-4 in the south. The 21st ARVN's mission was to root out the Viet Cong (VC) guerillas in the southwestern part of South Vietnam, an area vital to the nation as major fields of rice were grown in the low lying, flat, wet areas found there. The division had a good reputation for keeping the VC at bay but there was still work to be done to secure the area. Beyond that, the officer Ed talked with told him he would get more specifics when he got to Ca Mau, the town where the division's headquarters was located.

The following day after drawing some equipment, to include his M-16 and a .45 caliber pistol (he was more familiar with that weapon now), DeVos found himself on a C-7 Caribou, a twin engine rugged airplane that specialized in short takeoffs and landings. Its maximum load was thirty-two soldiers; two hundred miles per hour was the aircraft's maximum speed. The first stop on his journey to Ca Mau was at Can Tho, the MR-4 headquarters, one hour flying time from Saigon, the airfield on the western side of that town. As the C-7 made its final approach, the captain noticed a number of UH-1 Hueys, and further down the strip were some U.S. Navy planes, OV-10 Broncos, a twin propeller light attack plane, he learned were assigned to a light attack squadron. One of this squadron's missions was to support U.S. Navy elements, called the "Brown Water Navy," as these U.S. gunboats, sometimes called swift boats, patrolled the numerous rivers and tributaries of the Gong Hau River, part of the Mekong River complex whose headwaters began with the snows that fell in Tibet, twenty-seven hundred miles to the northwest, making the Mekong the twelfth longest river in the world. This Navy squadron, nicknamed "Black Ponies," also provided close air support to elements of the South Vietnamese Army to include the 21st ARVN. As Ed learned later, their ability to accurately put "steel on target" helped give them their slogan, "Down and dirty, low and slow," which was a God-send when the situation required their expertise.

Anxious to get to his final destination, the captain talked to a Navy officer in flight operations and hitched a ride on the next Huey heading to Ca Mau, an hour's flight time southwest. En route, the view from the helicopter verified the flat terrain of this part of South Vietnam, a mix of large open areas of rice lands, separated almost in squares by large mounds of mud and dirt dug from the fields, forming dykes which for long distances provided the only means to get out of the ever-present murky water. Large thick swampy areas seemed to be spread haphazardly around huge parcels of land reminding this Infantry officer of the Okefenokee Swamp in southeastern Georgia. The Vietnamese called this area the U Minh Forest, an unforgiving collection of vines, reeds, and large trees forming a thick jungle, home to big snakes, monkeys of every variety, and animals that thrived in this almost impenetrable, harsh, inhospitable world.

Upon arrival in Ca Mau, a jeep took him to the 21st ARVN compound and the headquarters of Team 51. The admin officer of the team, a major, quickly showed him where he could bunk and grab some chow, giving the new man instructions to return at 1600 to meet the Division Senior Advisor, Colonel (COL) J. Ross Franklin, who was currently in the field.

At 1550 hours, Captain DeVos returned to the headquarters and within five minutes he found himself seated in front of COL Franklin, a man with a gruff, gravelly voice and a haircut only Yul Brynner could admire. Through his many years as a professional soldier, this man had earned a shoulder full of awards, including the Distinguished Service Cross for actions as a Lieutenant in Korea. Now in his third tour in South Vietnam, he had served in the 173rd Airborne Brigade, the 82nd Airborne Division, and as the Deputy Chief of Military Advisor Command, Special Operations Group (MACSOG). He was Ranger Qualified, a rated aviator, a graduate of the French War College, and had been a member of the Peers Commission, the group that investigated the My Lai massacre. This 1950 West Point Class graduate was the most decorated member of his class. In DeVos' experience from days ahead, Ross Franklin was one of the best men he would ever know. He passed away in 2012.

During their short meeting, Ed understood he would be flying out the next morning to join the advisory team of the 33rd Infantry Regiment under the command of LTC Charles McClain who would then put this new officer with a battalion once he "got his feet on the ground." This was another way of saying, "Let's see how much potential and knowledge you have before we put you out there somewhere by yourself with some Vietnamese soldiers who have seen American advisors come and go for the last eight, nine years."

* * * * *

Early the next day, the new guy was on a Huey flying twenty minutes north to the 33rd Regimental Fire Base located along a major VC infiltration route, the Song Trem River. The fire base was in a large square area on dry ground next to the river. Fighting positions were located on all the mud and dirt walls of the dykes, facing out to provide cover if attacked. The fire base housed the regimental CP, two infantry battalions of the regiment, the 1-33 and 2-33, and the artillery battalion headquarters and two of its artillery batteries of 105mm howitzers for support. Four of the advisors, three captains and one Sergeant First Class (SFC), shared a makeshift shelter for sleeping and eating American rations. LTC McClain's housing was in another area near the regimental CP. One of the captains was the advisor to the artillery battalion and the two captains were advisors to the two infantry battalions in the fire base. The SFC was a swing man, able to help wherever the regimental senior advisor needed him.

LTC McClain's guidance to the new advisor was that he would give him a week or so to get his feet on the ground before McClain decided the best place to put him. Since things were fairly quiet, this would be a good time for the captain to watch, listen, and ask a lot of questions of his bunk mates. To start things off, McClain tasked him to teach a class on a night vision device the regiment had just received—the starlight scope. After two days of study, since he had never seen a starlight scope before, DeVos gave classes to four groups of twenty Vietnamese soldiers on how to use the scope. It was quite an experience as he would speak a sentence or two and then an interpreter would translate—how close the translation was to what the American said is anybody's guess. By the end of the third of four groups, the soldiers seemed to grasp the capabilities of what this new piece of equipment would do as the captain watched his audience closer, thinking more about them instead of his presentation.

As the first week slowly went by and without much to do, Ed had a discussion with one of the other captains who had been with the unit for only a month. It turned out this man, an armor officer, had seen no action since his arrival, and as these two without any experience in combat thought about that some more, they both realized it was possible that they could serve in this infantry unit for a year, and if they didn't get shot at, they could leave Vietnam without ever having been awarded a CIB, the award most Infantrymen treasure above all others. During their discussion, these two captains made the dumbest statement either would ever make—"I hope we get shot at enough times to get a CIB." Within a month, both of these officers would recall *how immature and plain stupid* they were in voicing such concerns.

* * * * *

On Christmas Day all the advisors with the 33rd Regiment were flown by Hueys back to Ca Mau for Christmas Dinner and a hot shower. They even got to spend a night sleeping on a real bed before they flew back to the fire base the next day. The next morning, LTC McClain instructed DeVos to pack what little he had as he would be flying out later that day to be the battalion advisor to the 3rd Battalion of the 33rd Infantry Regiment. That battalion had its own fire base and was located right in the middle of the rice growing area nicknamed "The Rice Bowl," halfway between the Song Trem River and the Gulf of Thailand; seven kilometers (clicks) west of the regimental fire base in one direction and the seven clicks east of the Gulf of Thailand in the other direction. Major Chan was the battalion commander of 3-33 Infantry and he also had one battery of 105mm howitzers to support the unit. The mission of 3-33 Infantry was to interdict all VC traffic through the Rice Bowl and keep the Vietnamese citizens who lived in that rice growing area free from VC interference. The SFC on the regimental team and an interpreter would accompany DeVos.

Later that afternoon the three men hopped off a Huey in the middle of the Rice Bowl at the fire base and met Major Chan. This man was an average looking Vietnamese in stature—about five foot six and thin, but his eyes had the look of cold steel. In later conversations, DeVos learned that Chan, thirty-one years old, had been fighting the VC for over half his life. He spoke broken English, far better than the U.S. captain spoke Vietnamese, but through the interpreter, a young soldier who had learned English four years ago, they were able to communicate easily.

As he walked around the fire base, a place that would be his home for the next three months, the advisor noted that, like the regimental fire base, this one was in the shape of a square, and it sat next to a good size stream, its water flowing slowly west toward the Gulf of Thailand. There were numerous places on the dirt and mud filled dyke walls where the soldiers could shoot from if attacked. The base of the walls on the inner side was around eight feet wide because the soldiers' families had staked their claim to that ground as their home. Cooking fires were every fifteen, twenty feet along the inner walls. Small children and wives of the soldiers were everywhere. Most knew no other life.

In the center of the fire base were six 105mm howitzers, two guns facing due north, two guns facing southeast, and the other two facing southwest; rounds for each of these artillery pieces were stacked up next to each gun, ready to fire. The helicopter-pad where the Huey put DeVos down was in the center of the firebase. There was a large ammunition bunker also near the center which Major Chan offered as the captain's sleeping quarters. With no other options readily available, the young advisor dropped his rucksack off there while the more experienced SFC said he would find some place along the wall.

The evening meal that first night was like so many others that followed: some thin tea followed by a bowl of rice in which sat the meat of the day. Sometimes that was fish, sometimes chicken, sometimes dog, sometimes monkey, or sometimes other delicacies of unnamed origin. Major Chan and others watched with great interest to see if this U.S. advisor, "*Co Van My*" in Vietnamese, would eat, because if he did, he would be offered a second helping. The Co Van knew if he rejected the meal or any of its contents, this could put a damper on his relationship with his host. Therefore, like it or not, eating whatever was put in front of him was part of the advisor's job. While he quickly became an expert at using chopsticks, some of these meals contributed to DeVos having diarrhea for long periods of time.

Over time two things saved his dietary system from irreparable damage. First, every time he filled his canteen with water, he dropped in a few halazone tablets. These tablets were first used in World War II for the same purpose Ed was using them; to disinfect the water. Second, after every evening meal, Major Chan always had several shots of his favorite drink, Hennessey Cognac, and like any good advisor, the young captain used this opportunity to bond with his counterpart.

This nightly custom helped stave off the taste and contents of such epicurean delights such as duck blood soup, twelve-day-old turtle eggs, or the various parts of the chickens that were chopped and cooked after all the feathers of the bird had been plucked and what was left was thrown into a big pot to become the chicken stew for the evening meal. There was also ever-present dipping sauce known as *nuoc mam*, the

Vietnamese fish sauce made from a combination of sugar, sweet and sour juices, garlic and various parts of fish.

As the weeks passed, on every occasion when Ed had the opportunity to get back to Ca Mau to get a shower, he would go by the small post-exchange (PX) located there to purchase more "medicinal" liquids for him and Major Chan to share. It was, after all, in the spirit of maintaining good rapport and proper international relations between these two men from different cultures.

The night in the ammunition bunker proved to be one this young infantryman would never repeat. No sooner had he gotten into the small entrance to lay out his camouflage sleeping blanket, which he still has in his possession fifty years later, and get his mosquito net strung up, he heard the scurry of small creatures in one of the corners of the ten-by-ten foot space. Thinking he scared whatever it was away, the man was stretching back down on his poncho when he heard the noise again, this time in two corners, then three, and in short order, he realized all those noises came from rats of varying sizes up to that of a small cat. After whacking a few of the invaders away with his entrenching tool, the racket grew worse as the creatures became bolder in their approach to this interloper who sought to occupy their space. Within thirty minutes, DeVos picked up his gear and found an open spot near one of the artillery pieces and tried to sleep, only to be interrupted in the middle of the night by a thunderous deluge from above.

The next morning, DeVos, after hardly sleeping a wink, was given a cup of thick, dark coffee by one of Major Chan's men, the coffee made according to French customs as their influence in Southwest Asia dated back to World War II and before. Feeling better with that hot liquid in his gut, this experienced battalion advisor of all of one day was about to take a "walk about" when Major Chan strolled over to him. With a big grin on his face, he told DeVos he found a spot where the American could bed down that evening which might be a little more comfortable.

In thinking about this as he walked around the fire base, Ed knew that, because he hadn't made a big deal of the previous night's experience with all the furry creatures visiting him, he had passed a vital test.

With every step around the perimeter, a new world opened up to the American. Small children followed him around, touching the hair on his arms, smiling at him as they laughed back and forth with each other as this man tried his best to speak Vietnamese. The wives of the soldiers he encountered along his walk kept bowing to him even as he bowed back. He noted several soldiers and some women along the river bank, the women washing their clothes while some of the soldiers were catching some fish ten or fifteen yards from those downstream who were using a cleared area along the bank as the camp latrine. When his bouts with "Montezuma's Revenge" were at their peak, the picture became clear. Human waste was eaten by the fish. Men caught those same fish to eat. Then men deposited their waste back into the water so the fish could eat, and then the cycle repeated itself. Since infantrymen are not known to be too bright, it took DeVos some time to fully comprehend this sequence.

* * * * *

During his second week at the firebase, DeVos had a discussion with LTC McClain when the regimental advisor flew in to see how the new guy was doing. Part of this conversation was that the LTC needed the SFC at another location. Without hesitation, the captain nodded his head in agreement saying he felt he could get along just fine without the SFC. Truth be told, Ed's assessment of this man was he was not any-where close to the professionalism shown by NCOs in 2-509 Airborne Infantry, and for the betterment of all concerned, when LTC McClain's bird lifted off later that day, the NCO in question was no longer at the firebase.

During the next few weeks, Ed went on several missions with Major

Chan's men. The first tromp he made in the woods was with a rifle company which was given the task to move toward the Gulf of Thailand looking for any signs of enemy movement, circling back to the fire base by a different route. While the company did not find anything on this six-hour mission, it was instructive to the advisor to see how these men moved in the woods, how alert they seemed to be, and to see the state of their physical fitness. In all these areas, the American felt good about what he saw. It felt good to get out of the firebase and pick fresh bananas off the trees they passed by. More importantly, he realized that he needed to get in better shape because his size ten jungle boots got sucked down into the mud so far, he struggled to pull his feet up fast enough to keep up with the soldiers near him.

The second mission DeVos went on was a squad night ambush. This was with ten men going out to set up an ambush five hundred meters outside the firebase on a trail the VC had been known to frequent. While no contact was made with the enemy that night, the advisor learned that the men he was with were quiet and disciplined. While it was difficult to assess how effective their weapons covered the kill zone, upon his return to the firebase four hours later, he had a new-found respect for the size and stings of the mosquitoes that owned the night sky in the Rice Bowl. This one night reinforced the need to follow orders and once a week take those giant-size malaria pills he had been issued.

Occasionally, U.S. Navy helicopters would fly over the Rice Bowl on their way to some ship out in the gulf. On one occasion, one pilot flying overhead radioed DeVos, asking him if he needed anything, to which the advisor responded that he had not had any ice cream in months. Within an hour, this Navy helicopter landed in the center of the firebase with a gallon of chocolate ice cream from some Navy ship. It didn't take too long to consume this feast in the ninety-five-degree heat.

In the midst of all this, one nagging administrative issue kept raising its ugly head. Just before Ed flew to Vietnam, the Army had updated its pay system to automatic bank draft. Complying with instructions, before deploying, the young captain filled out the paperwork so that he would receive fifty dollars a month and all the rest of his money would go directly to Susan's checking account in Florida. And you know the rest of the story. The Army reversed those instructions. It took several months of mailing money to Susan before all this got worked out, but it caused some concerns for the two of them at a time when there was enough stress in their lives.

* * * * *

By late January 1972, Ed had participated in several company-size airmobile insertions looking for any indications of VC movement. Several of those insertions woke up some VC and there were some small firefights, but nothing that amounted to much, although these small fights gave the advisor an understanding of what goes through your head when somebody is trying to kill you. These encounters laid to rest any concerns he had about getting a CIB.

In mid-February, LTC McClain and Col Franklin felt that this twenty-four-year-old advisor had enough experience that it was time for him to command a "Cav Pac" mission. This was a mission designed to ferret out the VC using the American aviation assets Ed had seen when he flew into Can Tho back in December. The helicopters used in this operation were: one Huey designated as the command and control (C and C) ship which Ed would be in; two OH-6s, fast, very maneuverable, light helicopters each with a pilot and gunner; two AH-1s, Cobra gunships loaded with rockets and cannons; and five more Hueys which would be back at the firebase with eight or nine Vietnamese infantrymen on board each aircraft ready to fly immediately if called into action by the C and C.

These missions were always tense as things could go in a number of different directions very quickly. The mission began with the C and C flying about three thousand feet above the area to be searched. Then the OH-6s would go in at almost ground level looking for any enemy signs, and if they spooked the well-hidden VC, they would mark the target with smoke rounds and get out of the way so that the Cobras could put fire on the target. Simultaneously, with the discovery of the enemy locations, the C and C would order the Hueys, loaded with the infantrymen, to fly immediately to this location, inserting them to "develop the situation."

While the possibilities of what could happen were almost endless, the two most dangerous were: #1 — One or both of the OH-6s would take fire and one or both could get shot down. When that happened, because it would take too much time to launch the Hueys and have them arrive to extract the two-man crews, the C and C would spiral down from above into a probable hot LZ to pick up the airmen, sometimes wounded, while the Cobras provided fire support. #2 — One or both of the OH-6s would take fire and mark the target with smoke; the Cobras would shoot up the area, and the Hueys would land the infantry, but since the size of the enemy force was unknown, this small force of forty to forty-five ARVN soldiers might not be large enough to handle an enemy that wanted to stand and fight. After taking part in three of these missions, and having to take action with respect to pulling some crewmen out of a hot LZ (Option #1 above), DeVos always considered the OH-6 crews, normally young warrant officers, to be some of the most courageous men he had ever seen.

In early March 1972, the pace of VC activity picked up. To help determine what that meant, patrol activity by the 21st ARVN's units increased. During one of the 32nd Regiment's patrols, two American advisors were badly wounded by a nasty booby-trap called a "Chinese Claymore," an explosive device that pounded the two men with pieces of metal and glass. One of those wounded was Captain Mike Tesdahl, an officer who had been stationed with the 1-509 Airborne Infantry in Mainz at the same time Ed was there in the sister battalion.

A week or so later, DeVos was attached as the advisor to the Division Recon Company with the mission of going to the Nam Can peninsula, the southern-most part of Vietnam, about thirty miles south of the normal area of operation (AO). The mission in this part of the "Forest of Darkness" was to search for American POWs. Nick Rowe, the first America POW captured in 1963 had been held in this area in a four-by-six bamboo cage until he escaped and was rescued in 1968. With intelligence indicating there might be more Americans being held in this area, the Recon Company went in with the help from a detachment from MACSOG. While no POWs were found, the 21st ARVN soldiers found cages similar to the ones described by Major Rowe.

During this mission, DeVos learned to never underestimate the enemy's ingenuity or his cunningness. This lesson came through loud and clear as the recon element was moving through the thick jungle when, without warning, the point man fell into a five foot deep pit filled with water. After pulling the soldier out, the area was examined in detail and the soldiers soon discovered several more of these pits, all filled with water and with something else. Each was filled with a large number of good-size fish swimming around. It turned out to be a VC resupply point. All the VC had to do was walk by a pit, grab a few fish, and keep on walking; they had supper whenever they wished to stop, testifying to the enemy's creativity and ability to make do without many creature comforts.

It wasn't too long after this that the 21st ARVN's soldiers and their advisors went from concentrating on guerrilla warfare favored by the VC to a more conventional war fought by the North Vietnamese Army (NVA).

* * * * *

Ed's first four months in Vietnam were instructive in several ways. First, there is a cycle in armed conflict: moments of sheer terror followed by days so quiet you almost forgot why you were there. The more the soldier experiences this cycle and begins to understand it, the more he begins to train his senses that the violence of armed conflict is closer when the silence seems to approach its zenith. The quieter it becomes, the more your senses have to be ready to act. While this drains the nervous system, you can never afford to let your guard down.

Second, when fighting a guerilla war, soldiers would do well to digest the words penned by John Ferling in his book, *Almost a Miracle, The American Victory in the War of Independence,* where he writes, "…Guerilla warfare is often more barbaric than conventional warfare. Guerrillas lack the means of coping with prisoners, they are usually less disciplined than those in a conventional army, and whatever their ideological ardor, many guerillas are drawn to fight from an inveterate hatred of their foe and an engrossing eagerness to settle old scores."

The bottom line is never underestimate what a guerrilla force can or might do. Their thinking is as unconventional as their tactics. Assume they will do the unexpected, the unconventional, the unpredictable, the sudden surprise coming out-of-left-field.

Therefore, the best thing you can do is think like the guerrilla. Think outside the box. Put yourself in their shoes and open your mind to the various possibilities that they might consider. Fight the guerrilla by using guerrilla tactics, not by using conventional ones. Otherwise, as the Chinese have written about for many years, they will wear you down and you will die "a death by a thousand cuts." One of the best sources in learning how to fight a guerrilla war comes from Robert Rogers' 28 "Rules of Ranging," written in 1757 during the French and Indian War. While the wording has been modified over the years, the professional soldier would do well to practice Roger's rules, tactics, techniques, and standing orders during all training opportunities to prepare for the days when he would be facing the enemy.

Third, don't assume that all officers or Non-commissioned officers are created equal. While this may appear to be obvious, the more experience you have working with men of all ranks, the more you will understand the implications of never assuming too much. It pays big dividends to ask questions, listen carefully to the answers you get, and don't ignore your gut when it tells you to double-check something. The more time you spend with soldiers of all ranks, the more valuable your gut feeling will be to your success as a leader. If something does not seem to be right, it probably isn't.

5. VIETNAM. THE 1972 NVA EASTER OFFENSIVE

Late March and early April 1972 has been labeled by historians as the start of the Easter Offensive, the North Vietnamese Army's (NVA) massive attack into South Vietnam. The offensive lasted almost four months. This was the second of three major offensives undertaken by the NVA during the Vietnam War; the first was the Tet Offensive in February 1968 and the third was the Spring Offensive that began in mid-December 1974 which ended in April 1975 with the North Vietnamese Army's taking of Saigon.

The Easter Offensive began 30 March 1972 when the NVA attacked in the Military Region-1 (MR-1) area toward Quang Tri and Hue. In MR-3, the enemy attacked Loc Ninh on 4 April which would then open the door for their push to capture An Loc, the provincial capital sixty-five miles north of Saigon. If the NVA captured An Loc, it was clear Saigon would be their next target. In MR-2, the NVA's target was Kontum. In total, the NVA committed fourteen divisions to these attacks. Because most American combat units had been withdrawn earlier in 1970 and 1971, the only major units that stood in the way of an NVA victory were the South Vietnam Army (ARVN) and their American advisors, some U.S. Army aviation units, and U.S. Air Force assets available to support the South Vietnamese.

* * * * *

By 7 April, the NVA's assault overwhelmed the ARVN forces at the town of Loc Ninh, despite the heroic efforts on the part of the U.S. advisors stationed there, and were moving rapidly toward An Loc, fifteen miles to the south. Standing in their way was the 5th ARVN Division and elements of other units that were rushed to this provincial city. Simultaneously, the 21st ARVN was alerted to deploy from MR-4 with the mission to move to Lai Khe, a town forty-five miles south of An Loc, and attack north up Highway 13 to relieve and/or reinforce the ARVN units defending An Loc to stop the NVA advance.

Movement orders were quickly issued and within twenty-four hours, the entire 21st ARVN was moving first to the airfield at Ca Mau before flying in an untold number of C-123s, C-7s, and C-130s to the sprawling airfield of Bien Hoa, sixteen miles north of Saigon. DeVos was on one of those C-123s that flew from Ca Mau to Bien Hoa on 8 April, the airplane loaded with soldiers and their families with all their earthly possessions; not just children, but bedrolls, makeshift tents, and in some cases, their goats and chickens. Because these aircraft were making multiple flights to and from Ca Mau, feathers and various animal deposits were scattered on the floors of these airplanes. After landing at Bien Hoa, everything and everybody was loaded on trucks and driven twenty miles to Lai Khe where the 21st ARVN CP was located. The orders at Bien Hoa were sketchy. In a nutshell, the word was once you get to Lai Khe, you will get your orders.

Once the 33rd Infantry Regiment arrived at Lai Khe, the situation became a bit more clear but there were still many unknowns: the NVA were attacking An Loc with a vengeance; the two or three NVA divisions in the An Loc area were reinforced with some tanks and a great number of indirect weapons, including some 105mm artillery pieces they had captured at Loc Ninh. The initial mission of the 21st ARVN was to attack north along Highway 13 to take some of the pressure off An Loc. There was no information about how many NVA units were near Highway 13 or what their strength was. The enormity of the situation and the fluid nature of intelligence and other information added to the confusion everyone felt in those first few days in Lai Khe.

* * * * *

After a day or two, the division hierarchy figured out a plan and DeVos found himself with 2-33 Infantry moving north, paralleling Highway 13 in a movement-to-contact mission. The switch for him from 3-33 Infantry to another battalion became common place within the 21st ARVN advisor team during the next three months as long-term members of Team 51 finished their one year tour in Vietnam and rotated back to the States, or as advisors got a break from combat and went on R & R (Rest and Recuperation), or as team members were wounded or killed. It was not something to be too concerned about, and as Ed reminded himself as he and his interpreter moved along twenty-five meters from the 2-33 Infantry command group, Ted Jenes from 2-509 Airborne Infantry days was right. What was needed now was patience, flexibility, and keeping your sense of humor when you can. For the next three months, all three phrases were lived out in many ways.

As the battalion commander of this battalion and his advisor quickly realized, the upcoming battles would be different than those experienced in the jungles of U Minh and around the Rice Bowl. The ground for the most part was dry and dusty. The trees in this part of Vietnam were sturdy as this area of operation (AO) was on the outskirts of the large Michelin Rubber Tree Plantation. There were some wet areas but not like what the unit was used to. The terrain for the most part was fairly flat with an occasional bump in the ground. The land adjacent to Highway 13 was devoid of much vegetation, evidence of Agent Orange. Scattered about were some large holes, fifteen to twenty feet across, six to eight feet deep. These were bomb craters, evidence of when the U.S. First Infantry Division prowled through this ground from 1967 to 1970. Most importantly, the enemy forces they would be facing were much different. This was not going to be guerrilla war. In this battle, the men facing them were a heavier force, possibly armed with tanks, and indirect fire support of every description, from mortars and rockets to long range artillery tubes up to 152mm. It would be a conventional fight, one not seen like this before in Vietnam.

The 2-33 Infantry's mission was to find the enemy, fix him in place, and then destroy him. Because this was the first time the battalion would be in this area, it was expected to be a movement of four kilometers north on the west side of Highway 13; then cross the road, and then return to Lai Khe on the east side of the highway. This was the second battalion to undertake this particular mission. The day before, a battalion from the 32nd Infantry Regiment had moved through this same area and had made no contact. It seemed like it would be a good shake-down for the battalion to get the "kinks out" and get some familiarization of the terrain. All the intelligence sources, both U.S. and Vietnamese, indicated that the NVA units were concentrated around An Loc, far to the north.

The mission began as briefed. The soldiers moved well with good spacing between individuals and units. As Ed strolled along near the battalion's command group, he suddenly realized he was being followed. There were two reporters from Pacific Stars and Stripes Magazine, a newspaper published by the Armed Forces, who were trying to catch up with him. Once they got closer and after a very brief introduction, he suggested to them that this might not be the best place for them to look for a story, but they insisted that they would not get in the way. They had driven up from Saigon for the day and had been given the task of "finding the war" since it was now getting closer to Saigon. These two tucked in behind DeVos and his interpreter for the next several hundred meters. It was almost like a walk in the park when …

* * * * *

The movement of the 21st ARVN Division to Lai Khe was no secret to the NVA as their intelligence gathering was always first rate. With their plan to move down Highway 13 toward Saigon after they took An Loc, advance elements of one NVA division were already in place ready to secure this major road. As the 21st ARVN began to move toward An Loc, the NVA began a series of counterattacks to halt that advance.

Fights were vicious and progress by the 21st ARVN was slow despite the grit shown by the ARVN soldiers and their leaders. There were many occasions when the NVA units used civilians as shields. Once the battle was joined, each step 21st ARVN soldiers took was met with barrages of mortar and artillery fire which could only be effectively countered by U.S. and Vietnamese Air Force (VNAF) airpower as the NVA had more fire support. Because the basic tactics initially were to move north by paralleling Highway 13, ARVN units were easy to track and the NVA took full advantage of this. This all became obvious during that first movement-to-contact.

* * * * *

…Well camouflaged NVA forces of an unknown size opened up on lead elements of the battalion with machine guns and observed 82mm mortar fire. The 2-33 Infantry soldiers reacted well, finding some cover behind the large ant hills that seemed to be everywhere and immediately returned fire. With the element of surprise, the NVA had the initial advantage. While they made no effort to attack, from the accuracy of their mortars, it was obvious they had forward observers watching the battalion's every move.

As DeVos and his interpreter, who was carrying the radio, moved to where they could see, within a few moments the advisor was talking to a forward air controller (FAC) flying in the general area who quickly answered his call. Soon the FAC was overhead and getting a better feel for the situation as he was contacting U.S. aircraft to fly to his location on one radio even as he talked to Ed on a different radio. These transmissions between the guy on the ground and the FAC helped the FAC get a better feel for the tactical situation and get specific locations for the "good guys" as well as the enemy's location.

Upon request, identifiable terrain features were passed to the FAC and friendly units marked their positions with colored smoke grenades. The FACs whose call signs were Rash, Covey, or Sundog, would then brief the inbound aircraft of both the friendly and enemy locations. When they were on station, the FAC would dive, fire smoke rockets to mark the target, and then tell these aircraft when they were cleared in "hot." Only then would these fast or slow movers roll in and drop their ordnance. After each bomb run, the guy on the ground would tell the FAC where to move the next set of bombs, i.e. "north one hundred meters" or "same place." This would be the basic pattern for the air support in this battle and all that followed.

The variety of aircraft to make these air strikes was impressive: "fast movers" or jet fighters available were F-4 Phantoms, F-8 Crusaders, A-7 Corsairs, A-4 Sky Hawks, and/or F-105 Thunder Chiefs. The employment of B-52s, C-130 Specter gunships, and AH1Cobra Gunships will be addressed later. Slower but more accurate airplanes employed were A1E Sky Raiders and A37 Dragonflies. Ordnance normally available on these aircraft were "dumb" or unguided bombs such as the Mark 81, weighing two hundred and fifty pounds, up to the Mark 82 weighing five hundred pounds, cluster bomb units, rockets, cannons, machine guns, and napalm. Ed, along with most of the other advisors, favored the A1Es and the A37s because, not only were they more accurate because they flew at slower speeds, they carried more ordnance and they could loiter on station for longer periods of time as compared to the faster jets who burned up gas quicker.

When an aircraft appeared overhead, ready to lay down fire on the enemy, the men on the ground were always glad to have them show up, regardless of the ordnance they carried. Virtually every air strike DeVos put in was classified as "Danger Close" meaning the friendly forces were within two hundred and fifty meters or less of where the aircraft would be dropping their ordnance. It was clear right from the beginning the primary role of the U.S. advisors in this fight would be to provide that critical link to the awesome power available through the U.S. Air Force, Navy, Marine, and the Vietnamese Air Force (VNAF).

After the airmen dropped their ordnance, the man on the ground would almost always give them a good report of their bombing accuracy and effect, called a bomb damage assessment (BDA) because he wanted the flyboys to come back as it was good for both the pilots' morale as well as for those on the ground. Even if the bombs did not hit the exact target, the guys on the ground knew the noise of those airplanes scared the crap out of the bad guys. Sooner or later, the pilots above would radio, "I'm Winchester" or "I'm RTB." Winchester meant the pilot was out of ordnance. RTB meant he was returning to base; he was out of fuel. Either way, the guys on ground no longer had air support until the next set of airplanes showed up. Depending on the tactical situation, the waiting could be quite nerve-wracking.

* * * * *

...After the air strikes went in, there was a noticeable reduction in the enemy fire hitting the battalion, and so the unit moved cautiously forward and found evidence of the destructive power of the airstrike. The 2-33 Infantry commander was then ordered to keep looking for the enemy, which resulted in the battalion remaining overnight in the AO. Around midnight the NVA lobbed some intermittent harassing mortar rounds to keep everyone awake and on edge. Early the next morning, hungry and wet from an overnight thunderstorm, the battalion returned to Lai Khe with a bit of a swagger in its step. As for the Stars and Stripes guys who were following Ed, they left soon after the bullets started flying, although they got some pictures and did several stories on what they saw that day.

* * * * *

This one engagement described above typified the day-by-day fights units of the 21st ARVN had for most of April and going into May: sharp, close in fights with NVA conventional forces, armed with a number of indirect fire weapons. As the units of the 21st ARVN attempted to leap-frog up Highway 13, both by foot and by helicopter assaults, the NVA grudgingly gave up two steps before taking back one, day after day. While many of the other missions experienced varying degrees of intensity, two fights require some elaboration.

The first was when one battalion in the 32nd Infantry Regiment was overrun late one afternoon. The exact circumstances were sketchy, but losses were heavy and the battalion advisor of that unit, Captain Hank Faldermeyer, was killed in the attack. Like all the rest of the infantry battalions in the 21st ARVN, Hank was the only American with that unit. His loss was felt throughout Team 51 as each battalion advisor like Captains Dewey George, Pete Nielson and DeVos knew that what had happened to Hank could happen to them as well.

The second engagement of note came as the NVA continued to interdict all movement along Highway 13, resorting to using civilians as human shields as these non-combatants attempted to flee from the battles raging all around them. One of these fights became known as the "Battle of the Blue Bus," where a bus loaded with civilians was attempting to move south from Chon Thon, the largest town located between An Loc and Lai Khe. The NVA stopped the vehicle, clogging up the road, and held positions around the bus for some distance, using the civilians who were attempting to get out from the war as human shields, preventing elements of both the 32nd Infantry Regiment north of the bus and the 33rd Infantry Regiment south of the bus from attacking.

The NVA hammered both regimental units with both indirect and direct fire weapons while the ARVN battalions, one of which DeVos was with, could only make incremental movements forward for fear of hitting innocent men, women, and children as well as firing into friendly forces. During this fight, Ed's Vietnamese interpreter was wounded and he was never replaced, making communications with his Vietnamese counterpart a little dicey at times. After five or six days of making slow, painful strides, the NVA melted away one evening, leaving behind a number of civilian causalities.

During this particular battle, DeVos and those Vietnamese near him came under a heavy mortar attack as you could hear the many rounds come out of the mortar tubes — Pop, Pop-Pop … Pop-Pop … Pop … Pop-Pop. Fortunately, there were a number of bomb craters nearby which they jumped into for protection. To the uninitiated, a mortar round can be heard as it descends if it is within fifty meters or so of your location — the whistling sound you hear is from the fins on the back of the round spinning. On this day, those other eight or nine men with the advisor in this bomb crater heard a lot of whistles.

Miraculously, none of those rounds landed in the crater, all hitting within ten to fifteen feet from the hole, because if one or two of those had landed in the crater, this paper you are reading would not have been written. After taking a quick look around and assessing the situation, as soon as the second set of Pop—Pops came, all of those in the holes made a mad dash for the nearby wood line, ignoring one of General George Patton's World War II dictums which suggested that infantrymen under a mortar attack should advance rapidly toward the mortar fire, not away from it. While General Patton's thoughts make good tactical sense, on that day and at that time, discretion won out over valor.

Editor's comments: The following are abbreviated comments that appear on the Silver Star citation presented to Captain DeVos in June 1972:... (During the period 23 to 28 April 1972) The enemy (was) fighting with unusual tenacity repeatedly through mortar, rocket, machinegun, and small arms fire ... inflicting heavy casualties upon friendly forces. Captain DeVos was with the lead elements of the 2nd Battalion of the 33rd Regiment in exposed positions to actively and aggressively ... direct(ed) tactical air strikes while receiving almost continuous direct and indirect fire. (His) demonstrated courage and physical stamina contributed ... to his battalion's ability to make repeated assaults in the face of devastating fire (to help) the battalion attain a link-up ... after six-days of intense, bitter combat.

* * * * *

By the middle of May, the NVA still maintained a great deal of pressure on An Loc, but something had to give as there was no roadway open to that beleaguered city. All the resupplies for the ARVN forces trapped in An Loc came by airdrops and there was no artillery in range to provide fire support, meaning all their fire support came from U.S. airpower with some help from VNAF aircraft. A bold plan was hatched to try to help break this impasse.

In mid-May, DeVos accompanied 1-33 Infantry on a mission to make a night move to get around the NVA positions along Highway

13 north of Chon Tanh by going due east of the highway for three or four thousand meters, then turning north for ten thousand meters before turning back to the west to occupy the village of Tan Khai located south of An Loc. The purpose of this move was to set up an artillery fire base to give fire support to An Loc and along ARVN movements along Highway 13 to augment the close air support that was keeping An Loc from being overrun.

This battalion, now numbering around less than three hundred men because of losses the last month, had never done any night moves prior to this mission, at least none higher than squad level. The move began to the east with about one hour of daylight remaining. Once it turned dark, the move became a major cluster. Many voices, noises, and rattles of all kinds, flashlights, numerous stops and starts for navigation checks were made as the night wore on. As Ed described it later, it was the Ranger patrol from hell. Somehow or maybe through sheer blind luck and God's intervention, the NVA didn't make any moves against the battalion, probably because they simply had no idea that it was bumbling around in the woods some distance east of Highway 13. With about two hours of darkness remaining, the battalion commander made the turn to the west toward Tan Khai, halting several kilometers from their objective.

After quiet settled in all around the tired and weary soldiers, without warning, one of the M-60 machine gunners on the perimeter opened fire. It was quickly discovered that there was nothing out there; the soldier just got spooked. As soon as dawn came, the battalion commander gathered all his men around him and pistol-whipped the soldier for a minute or so as he explained to the rest of the battalion that this one man's actions could have cost a great number of lives if the firing of that weapon had alerted the NVA of the unit's location. His object lesson was simple. Don't give away your crew served weapons positions until there is a genuine need. And the U.S. advisor understood: his counterpart handled this lesson in a way appropriate to his culture, and without question, the soldiers of the battalion got the point their commander was making. Without another word, the men saddled up and occupied Tan Khai later that morning without a shot being fired.

Within several hours of the occupation of Tan Khai, a significant roar from the south could be heard as six CH-54 Sky Cranes with a large gunship support element came toward the village at two thousand feet. Under each Sky Crane was a 105mm howitzer. Other helicopters in this air flotilla carried the artillery crews and ammunition. After unloading these artillery pieces, within an hour the ARVN artillery unit began to receive fire missions to support the friendly forces in An Loc.

While the idea behind taking Tan Khai and making it a fire support base made sense, the NVA were not blind and certainly not stupid. There was no way they had not seen or heard the massive, noisy Sky Cranes flying at two thousand feet with an artillery tube on a sling underneath. Within two hours the village began to receive effective artillery and mortar rounds from everything and anything in the NVA arsenal. Their initial target was the artillery battery. The ground shook as hundreds of rounds came flying in. Intermixed with mortar fire came larger shells fired from 122s, captured 105s from Loc Ninh, and everything in between. These larger indirect weapons made different sounds than mortars. First, you could hear the rounds come out of the tube, and when you heard that sound, you had only a few seconds to hit the ground and take cover because the shrieking roar of the round came to your ears for only a brief moment before the round hit. Sometimes the crashes sounded like a hundred cases of Coke bottles hitting the floor after having been dropped from a thousand feet. Some rounds sounded like a runaway locomotive flying toward you. Some landed with a sharp CRACK as the shrapnel whizzed by.

The destruction and sounds from those big guns made that day were something those who lived through it would never forget. DeVos was told later by some intelligence guy that the NVA fired five thousand rounds of varying weapons at Tan Khai during a four day period. While the source of that information is unknown, no one who survived those days would argue with that number.

By nightfall, four of the six 105s that had been brought in by the Sky Cranes were completely destroyed and the remaining two could be moved about only with great effort. Two hours later, those on the north side of the perimeter, the side facing toward An Loc, could hear the distinctive noise of tracked vehicles coming closer and closer. Knowing that the NVA had tanks, everyone went on full alert. Hurried radio calls on both the Vietnamese and U.S. advisors radio channels provided no information as to the tracked vehicles that were getting closer and closer to Tan Khai. Were these friendly or were they NVA?

With no indication about who or what might be closing in on the village that dark night, the commander of 1-33 Infantry ordered the two remaining 105s that could still shoot to prepare to engage the oncoming force by direct fire. The minutes ticked by until there was no time left. A decision had to be made. And with that, the two guns opened fire, killing ten or so wounded South Vietnamese soldiers who were being transported to Tan Khai from An Loc. Somehow, the friendly units around An Loc had gotten a hold of two M113 personal carriers and were making a run for safety. This fratricide incident could have been avoided if those at Tan Khai had been alerted to look for these men. The linkup would have been difficult, but not impossible. Unfortunately, things like this happen in the fog of war.

* * * * *

The battle of Tan Khai lasted four days. NVA ground attacks came each day, each preceded with bugles blowing at various times from all directions of the compass as they had the ARVN soldiers and their one advisor completely surrounded. The soldiers of 1-33 Infantry were well dug in and managed to stop the ground attacks every time. It was close on several occasions but the non-stop flow of U.S. and VNAF aircraft made the difference, all directed by the FACs overhead from dawn to dusk coordinating with the U.S. advisor on the ground. By the third day, resupply of both food and ammunition was necessary so bundles of the needed supplies were dropped by parachute by C-130s from ten thousand feet. Eighty per cent of what was intended for the Vietnamese soldiers in Tan Khai fell into NVA hands. The food resupply turned out to be canned tuna fish and dry rice in large sacks. With very little water available to add to the rice, the stomachs of the soldiers were put to the test.

As darkness came upon the village each evening, the ability to receive close air support shifted from the FACs to C-130 "Specter" Gunships who communicated directly with DeVos. The "Specter" was and still remains in use today because of its unique weapons platform. During the time of this battle in 1972, these gunships carried a 20mm cannon and a 105mm howitzer that fired from one side of the aircraft. Most importantly, the crew of the aircraft had the ability to identify targets on the ground from an altitude of ten thousand feet with infrared technology. The lethality of this aircraft was clear to Ed one evening when the NVA attempted a night attack and he forwarded their location to "Specter" in six-digit grid coordinates which meant he located the target on the ground to within one hundred meters. But once the crew of the gunship locked in on those coordinates, through their sophisticated equipment, the crew called the American back to confirm the target using eight-digit grid coordinates which meant that they spotted the target to within ten meters of its actual location. When "Specter" opened fire a few moments later, the NVA attack was stopped in its tracks by a rain of fire from above. To this day, DeVos believes the enemy never knew what hit them.

* * * * *

Once the NVA finally pulled back from Tan Khai in late May 1972 after the beating they had received from the airstrikes, DeVos was able to get to the site of a Cobra crash several clicks north of Tan Khai. This helicopter was shot down while 1-33 Infantry was surrounded in Tan Khai as it was escorting a Medivac helicopter to An Loc to pick up a wounded U.S. advisor. Those in Tan Khai witnessed the shoot-down from a distance and from what they saw, this was one of the first, if not the first time, the NVA employed a Russian SA-7 or Strella, a sophisticated, shoulder-fired, surface-to-air guided missile. Upon reaching the crash site, Ed found the body of one of the two crewmen but there was no sign of the second man. Several hours later, upon his return to Tan Khai with the remains of the one airman, a Huey piloted by COL Franklin flew in to take this American service member home. During this evacuation, DeVos and those with him were literally pulling civilians off the skids of the helicopter so it could get airborne. The ultimate whereabouts of that one missing airman still haunts Ed to this day.

Editor's comment: The following are some abbreviated comments made on the second Silver Star citation Captain DeVos was presented in June 1972:... (During the period 20 to 24 May 1972) the 1st Battalion of the 33rd Regiment... (was) repeatedly subjected to intense regimental size ground attacks supported by mortar and artillery fire. Captain DeVos... repeatedly exposed himself to enemy fire... in preparation of the base defense... continuously under fire... from which he could request and direct devastating air strikes... working throughout the period almost without sleep and it is doubted that without him, the only U/S. advisor present, that the base at Tan Khai could have been held by friendly forces. His... accurate direction of air strikes (was) crucial to the successful defense of the Tan Khai base.

* * * * *

With the way to An Loc now beginning to show signs of opening, a battalion from the 32nd Infantry Regiment came into Tan Khai as 1-33 Infantry moved north closer to An Loc in early June 1972, almost reaching the rubber trees signaling that the city was seven or eight kilometers away. As the unit came under intense fire, it was forced to dig-in on a ridgeline facing the enemy in a broad front, and after several hours of sharp contact and calling in a number of airstrikes which seemed to have no real impact on the situation, it was apparent more serious measures would be required to break this stalemate, and so DeVos asked over the radio if an Arc-Light strike could be flown in this area. This was also a bitter-sweet time as another officer had been designated to be Ed's replacement with the battalion. This man was an LTC artillery officer, who had a lot of staff time in Vietnam and who had requested that he be sent forward to get some combat experience. For several days he stayed close on the heels of the Infantry captain.

As early as 1965, Arc-Light strikes were part of the U.S. bombing strategy used in the Vietnam War. These missions were flown by B-52s stationed in Guam and were normally flown against targets in North Vietnam, but because of the strong push by the NVA in the 1972 Easter Offensive, Arc-Light strikes were employed around critical locations for the defense of An Loc and in Kontum to the north. These were three ship missions, each bomber carrying some mix of five hundred, seven-hundred and fifty, and one thousand-pound bombs. The B-52s were radar guided and would drop their ordinance at altitudes so high they could neither be seen nor heard on the ground, and so the first indication of the air strike in the target area was the sound of all these bombs hitting in rapid order. For those in the Arc-Light box, it must have felt like you were on the bottom floor of a fifty-story building when it is demolished. From a distance one could almost envision invisible huge pre-historic monsters running through the woods, tearing all the trees apart, tossing all their limbs and roots skyward, leaving behind the large holes with no pattern to them. Any enemy forces in the target area stood little chance of survival. The noise of the shock waves as the bombs gouged up the ground dulled the hearing for those more than a thousand meters away.

Because these strikes were controlled at headquarters well above the advisor's level, the request went through a number of command channels before it was approved. Once approval was given, the grid coordinates of the target box were rechecked. Requirements for these strikes were that the target box was to be at least one thousand meters from friendly forces. This was called the minimum safe distance or MSD. DeVos sent in the grid coordinates for the box, knowing that the NVA would be within five to seven hundred meters from the friendly Vietnamese forces, well within the MSD, but he did so, trusting that the bombers would be precise in the bombing and that by striking closer to the friendly positions, more NVA would be on the receiving end of the Arc-Light strike. As he learned later, he was not the only advisor who took some "liberties" of moving the box closer to friendly forces with respect to the MSD because of the enemy situation.

After the strike was made, the battalion was able to make progress although not as much as anticipated, proving once again, the ability of the human body and soul to withstand incredible stress and pain. Since his replacement was now on board, Ed was not with the unit as they moved forward. His R&R (Rest and Relaxation) to meet Susan in Hawaii for a week had been changed because of the ebb and flow of the battle, and therefore, COL Franklin deemed it appropriate that this advisor be given the opportunity to leave the battle for a week.

Ed and Susan were blessed to be together for a week in Hawaii. It had been a stressful journey for Susan because before she actually flew to Hawaii, she had been contacted three times by the Red Cross, each time causing her heart to stop not knowing what she might be told about her husband. Each of these calls told her the dates had to be changed, multiplying her concerns for Ed even more as she wondered what her husband was involved in. When they finally met, each tried to hold back the tears as each tried to be strong and courageous for the other, even as the stress and strain showed on their faces, For Susan, it took her a few seconds to recognize Ed as he was skin and bones, his eyes and face drawn tight.

* * * * *

Editor's comments: The following is Susan's perspective about their meeting for R & R:

"…Yes, the anticipation grew as I was on my way to see Ed, but the reality of not seeing that strong, well fit soldier of a few months ago was a situation I was not sure how I would react to and it seemed to over shadow that first moment of our reunion so much so that I truly did not recognize him.

The embrace—the kiss –the moment of really having each other enveloped in a hug was something we did not want to let go of.

Looking at him face to face instantly showed the effects of war. The stress, the strain, the lack of sleep, and the guarded secrets that I knew would not be revealed showed up in the silence and as we spoke to one another. It quickly became apparent that my many questions need not be asked and those that were may not be answered and maybe that was best, for I probably could not bear the fullness of what my husband was going through.

Was it a time of rest and relaxation? In some ways yes and in some ways no. Many events and many offerings of entertainment were planned but he could not fully engage into the transition of "our world" and the attention. It would take more than five days. He tried his best but that switch could not be flicked on so easily because his mind was elsewhere. Thus, R & R was "bitter sweet."

To say goodbye a second time, especially after seeing the deterioration physically and emotionally was very hard. The brave front on my side was camouflaged by all the courage I could pretend at that moment. Both of our "reassurances" were given as we held back many tears.

The flight back to Florida was lonely and somber. It was quiet, the joy suspended because all my questions came back again. Will I see him again? Will he come home whole? And when he gets home, will he be able to adjust easily as he integrates back into the household as husband and father? Will he carry memories deeply imbedded in his mind, not to be unearthed and allowed to be private, or will others try to pry too much information from him and hinder his adjustment to his next military assignment?

To try to be an encourager to family members was another challenge as the flight home continued. Gentle grace with not too many details seemed to be the best way to keep the picture of strength and not weakness in their mind, because that way hope stayed alive for us all. Only then could we face each day with much continued faith and prayer until he was back with us and away from the war zone.

* * * * *

When DeVos returned a week later, a few things had changed, some for the good, others not so. First, after being the Division Senior Advisor of the 21st ARVN for over a year, COL Franklin was replaced by COL Cohn; a good man certainly, but God broke the mold when He created Ross Franklin. Second, 1-33 Infantry and the other battalions of the Regiment were now getting closer to An Loc and the NVA were throwing everything in their dwindling arsenal to hold them back, but momentum was shifting to the ARVN side. It seemed with the passage of time, the siege of An Loc would soon be broken. Third, because of all his time in the fight, Ed along with several others who had been fully engaged for the last few months was reassigned to help run Team 51's Tactical Operation Center (TOC), coordinating units and fire support at that level. Fourth and the one most distressing was that while Ed was on R & R, LTC Charles Butler was killed at Tan Khai.

LTC Butler had been with Team 51 as COL Franklin's right-hand man for some time. Awarded the Distinguished Service Cross in Korea at a young LT, he was someone those who had less experience could always seek out for advice and counsel. With so many younger officers moving about with various ARVN battalions during the last few months, he would help out by giving some of the other team members a break. He was killed at Tan Khai when he was in the command bunker when it took a direct hit from an NVA artillery round. This was the exact location DeVos had spent a great deal of time when the NVA made their big push to destroy 1-33 Infantry when it defended that village.

* * * * *

Two days later in the early afternoon, COL Cohn approached DeVos and said he needed to have a word with him. The senior advisor then told the captain that he had just learned that the 33rd Infantry Regimental Commander, Colonel Kahn, had been killed in an NVA artillery strike and that the senior American regimental advisor was seriously wounded. Because of the regiment's success in the past few months, the President of Vietnam, Nguyan Van Thieu, wanted to give a State Funeral to honor Colonel Kahn. Since Ed knew the situation better than most anyone else, Col Cohn asked him if he would go back into the fight and get the Vietnamese colonel's body out. What else could the captain say but yes. An hour before dusk, he found himself onboard a Vietnamese Huey heading north toward the Regiment's CP along Highway 13, surround-ed by rubber trees and the NVA south of An Loc.

The Vietnamese pilot of the Huey flew fast and low, and the closer they got to the rubber, he guided the helicopter around the trees, not over them. Five minutes out from the LZ, the NVA opened up on the helicopter, the aircraft taking fire all the way in to the landing site. As the pilot put the ship down, the wounded American advisor was thrust on board but there was no sign of the body of Colonel Kahn. DeVos then hopped off the helicopter and told the pilot he would see him again at dawn the next morning and he would have the body of Colonel Kahn with him. The pilot nodded and took off, drawing more fire when he did.

Within five minutes, the advisor had found the body and arrange-ments were made with the acting Regimental Commander that the heli-copter would be back the next morning and that the advisor would then escort the body out. With those decisions made, it was still a long night without much sleep as incoming NVA artillery kept everyone on alert. The next morning the Huey was right on time and within a few seconds after he landed, DeVos and the body of this Vietnamese hero were on board, flying again around trees not over them, taking fire all the way out. Once they cleared the rubber trees, Ed noticed the "chip light" on the control panel of the helicopter was blinking, a sign that there might be a major problem with the engine. The pilot, too, saw the indicator light and five minutes later, he landed the bird in an open field. After making a quick visual inspection of the engine and other vital parts of the Huey, he looked back at DeVos with a "thumbs up," mouthing "We go now." Twenty minutes later they landed back at Lai Khe as both men gave a great sigh of relief. Since that day, Ed always says that this VNAF pilot was the bravest pilot he had ever seen.

Three days later, this advisor was one of the most junior men at the ceremony held in Saigon to honor one of the heroes of the South Vietnamese Army. It was an all-day event with numerous dignitaries in attendance. DeVos stood well behind the rows of seats and as he recalled many events of the past three months, he was simply glad to be alive.

* * * * *

Many articles, after-action reports, and several books have been written about the battle of An Loc. Among them is *The Battle of An Loc* written by James H. Willbanks. Some official sources say that the An Loc battle ended at the end of June 1972; others will note that the fighting continued along Highway 13 until late July. The net result of all those days of fighting can perhaps be best expressed on a monument erected by the people of An Loc which says in part, "An Loc remained free because South Vietnamese soldiers stood and fought when they had no other choice." Other reports added, "No one … (believes) that the South Vietnamese could have held had there not been American advisors (with them)." Another comment noted that the advisors "were the glue that kept the ARVN together." Two U.S. units were awarded Presidential Unit Citations for their part in this battle: Team 70, the advisor team with the 5th ARVN and the 229th Assault Helicopter Battalion of the 1st Cavalry Division, as both were engaged right from the start of the NVA's march on An Loc, refusing to yield to the enemy's pressure despite being outnumbered five to one.

As Willbanks notes in his book, "The 21st ARVN paid a heavy price in its attempt to open Highway 13 … Although (the division) was not able to open the road, it tied down an entire NVA division that no doubt would have turned the tide had it been used on An Loc itself … During the course of the effort to relieve the embattled city, the 21st ARVN sustained 662 killed and 3,381 wounded … five of the nine infantry battalion commanders and twenty-one of twenty-seven company commanders were killed or wounded. The U.S. advisors with the 21st ARVN also suffered, with four killed and eighteen wounded."

On the last night before the 21st ARVN and its advisor team began to return to MR-4 and the U Minh, those advisors who were left assembled to pay respects to their fallen comrades. Each of those in attendance contributed some alcoholic beverage of their choice and all the contents were poured into one big pot—whiskey, beer, gin, rum, bourbon, and Cream de menthe. Later that evening when the results of their many rounds of toasts brought forth a predictable outcome, the outflow was a nasty green color, prompting those who were there that night to believe that Cream de menthe was far more powerful than one could ever imagine.

* * * * *

The last four months Ed spent in Vietnam were melodramatic as both the North and South Vietnamese soldiers were licking their wounds and taking some deep breaths. U.S. forces continued to draw down as our country sought a way to withdraw and still "save face." DeVos, on the other hand, still had work to do as he was assigned to be the lone advisor to the 21st ARVN's Training Center at Bac Lieu, a provisional capital south of Can Tho. The Vietnamese personnel he spent time with there were tired and spent. Most of the soldiers and their leaders were simply going through the motions, and, to some extent, DeVos was like everyone else as the physical and mental strain of extended combat took its toll.

His quarters were with the Provisional advisor team in an old French compound. He was now eating American food and was able to take another leave, this time fourteen days back to Florida. After returning from this time with Susan and his daughter, Kristen, he spent four days in Saigon at a training meeting, the time there amounting to nothing of significance, with one exception. The ride to and from Saigon went out of Can Tho in a CH-47 Chinook helicopter capable of carrying around twenty-five to thirty soldiers. This daily flight never varied in time or route. The day after Ed returned from this meeting in Saigon, this same helicopter flying the same route was shot down by the VC or the NVA, killing all those aboard. The two immediate lessons were first, just because things were relatively quiet, it didn't mean the war was over, and second, complacency about flying the same route between Can Tho and Saigon violated one of the standing orders that every good Ranger knows. "Never march home the same way (you went out). Take a different way (back) so you don't get ambushed."

As he went back and forth each day to the Division Training Center, a decision weighed heavy upon this captain's shoulders. Should he stay in the Army; accept the orders which he had just received to go to Fort Benning, or should he get out? He and Susan had discussed this during his recent leave and she was leaving the decision to him. Over and over his mind kept thinking about those good, good men he had served, and how he would miss them and others like them if he left the service. The more he thought about men like Ted Jenes, Bill Edge, Ron Male, Paul Griffith, Skip Watson, Ross Franklin, Charles Butler, Hank Faldermeyer, and others, it did not seem right to leave them. Once that decision was made, he did not look back for many years.

* * * * *

In early December 1972, Ed flew to Saigon for his final out-processing and on the appointed day, he, along with another two hundred and fifty of his comrades in arms, boarded a charter flight, a "Freedom Bird" which would take them back to the "Land of the big PX." A few minutes into the flight, the pilot of the aircraft announced that they were "Feet Wet," military terminology meaning that the plane was now over the ocean, no longer over South Vietnam. The roar of joy of those on the airplane was loud and long for several minutes until it was replaced by quiet reflections which brought tears of sorrow to many as they thought about those who would never make this flight home.

After landing at Travis Air Force Base located near Fairfield, California, DeVos got transportation to the San Francisco International Airport to catch a flight to Florida. Like all the other GIs, he was wearing his uniform, decked out now with a number of medals. As he was waiting for a flight, he sat down next to a mother and her young son, judging the mother to be about his age and the young boy was maybe two or three years old. Within two to three seconds after the soldier sat down, this woman looked at him with great disdain written across her face, and, without a word, she pulled her young son from his seat and left. No words were exchanged between the man and the woman. It was a "Welcome Home" this soldier will never forget.

* * * * *

There were a number of lessons DeVos took away from those days from early April to December 1972 which will stay with him for the rest of his life, but there are three primary ones.

Like so many around him, Ed was in a situation where he had to grow up quickly; to sift through the important from the unimportant, and act on the best information possible, particularly as it related to the synchronization or coordination of fire power — not just the infantry on the ground but the air assets that were supporting him as well. Key to any successes achieved on the battlefield were the logistics and communications required to keep everything moving as needed and, these, too, required coordination. Complicating this was some language issues with the people around him which were multiplied by the stress and strain of combat. Mistakes were made but he learned that you do the best you can do, learn from your errors when you can, and move on. In extended combat, you have little or no time to dwell on the "coulda," "shoulda," or "woulda." That will come later in your nightmares.

Second, there are not enough words to tell of the courage and dedication DeVos witnessed of the pilots of untold numbers of air-craft—fixed wing, jets, helicopters, etc.—that supported him and the others around him. Against some horrific odds, they kept their cool and their eyes fixed on the target as they bored in to drop their bombs or land the soldiers on the LZ or picked up the wounded. Brave men all.

Third, as Ed sat in that "Freedom Bird" as it winged its way home, he was proud to be a part of the legacy of his father and others who had worn the uniform of their country in this war and the others before it. Every man on that "Freedom Bird" with him that day had made a choice: a choice to serve their country unlike other "men" who had dodged that obligation in some manner. For those who answered the call, they formed an ever-lasting bond with each other who served their country. They were all part of something much larger than themselves. Because of that bond, it is the charge to the living to never forget the dead.

That sentiment was perhaps best expressed some years later by LTC Steve Russell at his change of command ceremony in Fort Hood, Texas. Russell was the Battalion Commander of 1-22 Infantry, one of the unit's that captured Saddam Hussein in December 2003. At that ceremony, he was speaking about a different war at a different time and a different place, but his words apply to those who served in Vietnam as well.

On that day Russell said, "…Someday your peers will look back on their lives and wish they were you. When your nation called, it was you who answered. Regardless what people will make of your service or this war, no one can take away what you have achieved. Ever…And as the decades pass and we grow old together, we must remember not only what has been accomplished but what the cost was as well…Only we carry the memory of the fallen…It is we who know their faces, their smiles, their stories, and their sacrifice. They are now just a name, but as long as we have breath, they will live."

6. FORT BENNING, GEORGIA. ON THE ROAD TO PROFESSIONALISM

From the middle through the end of December 1972, it was a whirlwind for the DeVos family. Ed returned from Vietnam. The Palm Beach Post, the area's largest newspaper, interviewed him about his experiences in Vietnam. The DeVos' sold their home in Lake Worth, Florida. They celebrated Christmas on Christmas day and had the movers come and pack their belongings for shipment to Fort Benning the next day. Then they drove to Fort Benning the following day to begin the process of finding a place to live. Kristen, now nineteen months old, suffered the indignity of opening Christmas presents one day and watching them get packed the next. Such is the lot of a military family, then as now.

In early January 1973, Ed and Susan found a nice duplex rental less than five minutes from one of the post's back gates, this one near Sand Hill, fifteen minutes from main post, but as sometimes happens with military household shipments, their household goods were delayed for almost a month and so they stayed with some good friends from their 2-509 Airborne Infantry days. Once the shipment arrived, the DeVos's moved into the duplex and immediately became part of a small community filled with other military families. Even though they had left Fort

Benning three years earlier, it felt like home to return to the Home of the Infantry and area around it.

Because Ed was not scheduled to start the Infantry Officer's Advance Course (IOAC) until mid-March 1973, he was temporarily assigned to work in the Post Logistics office located on the sixth floor of Building Four, better known as Infantry Hall, which housed the headquarters of both the post and the Infantry School.

While minimal tasks were handed him because he was short-term help in the Logistics office, several opportunities came his way. First, there was a five-day temporary duty assignment (TDY) to Camp Shelby, Mississippi, near Hattiesburg, a training site for a number of National Guard and Army Reserve units and home to the Army's Weapons Effectiveness Laboratory (WEL). The purpose of this TDY was to provide input to the people running this lab concerning how bunkers could be built that could withstand direct hits from Russian indirect fire weapons, i.e. artillery. Since Ed and several others had been on the receiving end of a number of these type weapons in Vietnam, WEL wanted their opinions about the practicality of building hardened bunkers on the battlefield of the future.

While at Camp Shelby, Ed and others with him looked at many structures from both the infantry and engineer perspective, they recommended that to try and "bullet proof" every bunker like the French attempted when they built their Maginot Line in World War II, on the ever-changing, fluid, future battlefield, was simply not feasible in terms of money, time, and limited engineer assets. While structures might be built that could withstand most direct hits from a 155mm round, thereby saving lives like those of LTC Butler and those with him at Tan Khai, to build these hardened bunkers all over the moving battlefield was not a good use of finite assets. After voicing these concerns, DeVos never heard another word about this proposal.

A second and a far more worthwhile venture came about without having to leave Fort Benning. The Army Research Institute (ARI) for the Behavioral and Scientific Sciences based in Washington, D. C. had developed over a number of years a four-day program where they could take groups of twenty "subjects," and run them through a battery of intelligence tests, leader war-games, leadership in simulated emergency exercises, written and oral practical leadership and emerging leader exercises, in-box exercises, several self-insight and self-evaluation exams, and other psychological tests too numerous to count. The purpose of all these tests and evaluations was to be able to predict within each group of twenty who was the # one leader, then the # two leader, in order down to # twenty. For four days, DeVos was one of twenty CIB wearing infantry captains "quarantined" in some World War II buildings where everything he and his fellow officers did or said or wrote was recorded and taped. A secondary purpose of this process, as Ed learned later, was to help ARI develop an improved Office Efficiency Report (OER), the primary rating system of the officer corps, by capturing leadership comments that were lacking in earlier iterations of the OER form.

Historically, the ARI personal who evaluated the mounds of data collected on each "subject," were so good at analyzing the data, they were ninety-five percent accurate concerning the ranking of each group of the twenty they evaluated. Their methodology was time consuming as at least one PHD of Psychology or some other related discipline reviewed all the data on each individual, comparing it against all others in that particular group.

After several months of analyzing all the information, ARI then prepared a seven-page report on each individual before one of the PHDs debriefed each participant individually. In DeVos' case, it was a short meeting as his briefer told him only two things, both of which were so valuable to Ed that he has carried that information in his head ever since. The first thing was that when he spoke to any group, regardless of the size, almost all in the group he was speaking to would react positively to him and his manner of delivery. In other words, the ARI recommendation was simply. "When you are in front of people, just be yourself. Those you are speaking to will trust and believe in you." Second, the man told Ed that he reacted poorly to change. Therefore, the recommendation was that, knowing his mind would always react in that manner, when on situations when changing something was being discussed, he should not react too quickly. Rather, he should slow down and give his mind a chance to evaluate the possible advantages of making this change *before he opened his mouth*. To have that information so early in this captain's military career was invaluable.

* * * *

IOAC in 1973 was close to nine months long. It was designed to prepare captains to be infantry leaders at the company level as well as to fill staff positions at the battalion level. The two hundred or so men in DeVos' class, almost without exception, were Vietnam veterans. With Vietnam quickly being looked at as "the last war," the Infantry School was refocusing on stopping the greatest potential threat—a Russian attack against NATO (North Atlantic Treaty Organization) forces in central Europe. In recognition of that threat, almost all of the instruction in the tactics department focused on stopping the Russian hordes from coming through the Fulda Gap, the traditional avenue of approach used by large armies as they attacked from east to west before spilling onto the German country side. In 2005, the name of this course was changed to be the Maneuver Captain's Career Course, but the thrust of the instruction remained similar to the IOAC classes of earlier days. Only the battlefields have changed.

The Tactics Instructor who made the biggest impression on Ed during his IOAC class was Major Steve Siegfried, who years later was the Commanding General of Fort Jackson, SC. Day after day, this major would pose questions to the class about what a mythical Russian captain he called Clyde was doing to prepare his men to fight his American adversaries: "I wonder what Clyde is doing today. Is he getting his men ready to ram his tanks and his mechanized infantry through the Fulda Gap? I wonder how tough he is on his soldiers. Is he physically tougher than you? Better prepared mentally than you? I wonder if when you command your next rifle company, will you train your men harder than Clyde, 'cause if you don't train 'em better, and I mean a lot better, then Clyde's gonna whip you bad when he overruns your company as he sweeps through the Fulda Gap."

Major Siegfried then followed those questions and comments like those above by reminding the class that since Clyde badly outnumbered us, the infantry captains in this IOAC class needed to out-think and out-work the Russians every day. As DeVos listened, he was one of those who took to heart the instructor's challenge, realizing that combat in the next war would require unparalleled mental and physical preparation. So, when Ed's results on the next Physical Training (PT) Test showed there were some areas needing improvement, he restructured his workouts so that he practiced all the events on the PT test daily. Three months later, when he took the next PT test, he achieved a near maximum score. For the rest of his Army career, this infantryman gave this area of preparation the attention it deserved, always achieving maximum or near-max scores from that day forward.

During this time COL Franklin, who was now the Director of Tactics in the Infantry School, contacted Ed and invited him and Susan to join him one night for dinner at the Fort Benning Officer's Club. On the night they met for dinner after one round of drinks and before the meal was served, Ross was ready to tell Susan some stories about her husband's exploits in Vietnam. But before he could begin, she stopped him cold, telling this old warhorse that she didn't really need to hear too much about all that, so, Ross, being the gentlemen that he was, backed off. Later that evening this Infantry colonel noted that the Secretary of the Army, Robert Froehlke, was sitting at a table nearby. Since he knew the man personally, Ross dragged Ed over to meet the Secretary, and for the next ten minutes, this Infantry Colonel told Mr. Froehlke some of the stories he wanted to tell earlier.

* * * * *

In 1970, the total strength in the active U.S. Army was 1.3 million men and women. By 1975, the strength of the Army had dropped to seven hundred and eighty thousand, a reduction of over five hundred thousand soldiers. This reduction in force (RIF) occurred primarily because of our country's commitment to South Vietnam in 1973 was drastically reduced to almost nothing. Related to this decrease in manpower, the Army transitioned from a draft system to an all-volunteer force, nicknamed VOLAR (short for Volunteer Army), which was adopted in 1973. This reduction in the Army's overall strength also meant that the size of the officer corps would be reduced by one-third.

As one can imagine, this had a detrimental effect on morale in the officer corps. Specifically, in Ed's IOAC class of two hundred, sixty to seventy officers could expect to be released from active duty before graduation day. RIF boards were held at Department of the Army (DA) level to "select" those captains Army-wide whose service would no longer be required. When the lists were published, those 'selected' had sixty days to pack their bags and leave the Army, although a few men chose to remain in the Army as NCOs.

On the surface, this sounds cruel to force men out of the Army who had served their country honorably. However, the Army had no other options in order to meet the Congressional mandates imposed upon it and still meet its war fighting requirements around the world. On the plus side, because of the four RIFs DeVos' year group went through, the majority of those who were selected to leave the service were those with substandard OERs as compared to their contemporaries. From a practical sense, this process meant that the bottom third of the captains on active duty were released from active duty, thereby keeping the cream of the crop to help move the post-Vietnam Army forward.

The RIF process coincided with those who remained in DeVos' IOAC as they received orders for their next assignment. In Ed's case, his orders read that he would remain at Fort Benning and be assigned to the 3rd Battalion 7th Infantry, part of the 197th Infantry Brigade (Separate), located on Kelly Hill, five miles from the heart of the post. Knowing that they would be staying at Benning for an extended period of time, the De-Vos' made the decision to buy a home in Columbus and move in as soon as possible. It was quite a gift. It turned out that their next-door neighbor was Captain Lanny Bassham, a member of the U.S. Army's Marksmanship Team. In the 1972 Munich Olympics, he won a Silver Medal and in the 1976 Olympics in Montreal, Lanny won a Gold Medal.

Included in Ed's orders was that prior to signing into 3-7 Infantry, he would be attending a special four-week course in Infantry Hall called the Nuclear Weapons Course or Prefix 5 Course. This meant that this captain spent the month of January 1974 after graduating from IOAC learning the ins and outs of the nation's nuclear weapons and how to employ and target them. It was quite an eye-opening experience as he took from Prefix 5 an understanding about how our Armed Forces go to great lengths to protect non-combatants to the maximum extent possible. Locations of significant civilian populations were always considered in the size of the nuclear weapon to be used and where it was to impact to inflict minimum civilian casualties and still destroy the intended military target in question. Unfortunately, these types of calculations did not seem to be of much concern to other countries who either had a nuclear capability or who were seeking to obtain such weapons at some future date.

* * * * *

Taken as a whole, 1973 was a transitional year for Captain DeVos. Now twenty-six, he had served his country for over four years and had committed to making it a career. He knew what risking life and limb was about. He had seen others give the ultimate sacrifice for their convictions. He was prepared for what the future might hold, and from all indicators, more would be expected of him in the days ahead. In short, he was no longer just along for the ride. He was becoming, if he wasn't already, a professional soldier. He was serious about his profession. Focused, thinking ahead, not just reacting to situations and problems around him. Others seemed to respect his thoughts and ideas. His reading interests turned to books about men like Lee, Grant, Chamberlin, Jackson, Rommel, Patton, Guderian, and Hannibal. *On War* by Clausewitz and Sun Tzu's work, *The Art of War* sat on his bookshelves.

He certainly didn't know everything he needed to know, but he had a good feel for what he didn't know. He looked forward to his assignment in 3-7 Infantry, knowing that he would be with Infantry soldiers again. That is where he longed to be. To lead them. To love them. To teach them. To learn from them. To be around them. To be challenged by them to do his best. It would be the highest honor. To be with such men again.

7. FORT BENNING, GEORGIA. DAYS OF LEARNING

The 3rd Battalion of the 7th Infantry Regiment was one of four battalions that was part of the 197th Infantry Brigade headquartered on Kelly Hill in 1974. The other battalions were the 1-58 Infantry (Mechanized), 2-69 Armored, and 2-10 Field Artillery. Included in the brigade structure were all the other combat support and combat service support units that would be needed if the brigade deployed. During the 1991 Gulf War, the 197th Infantry Brigade fought with distinction as part of the 24th Infantry Division.

Before DeVos signed in to 3-7 Infantry, he did his homework, learning about the 7th Regiment's historic past. Activated in 1812, the unit first fought at the Battle of New Orleans under the command of General Andrew Jackson who later was elected as our seventh President. During that battle, the unit positioned itself behind cotton bales as they fought the British. The cotton bale is now the centerpiece of the unit crest with the Latin words *Volens et Potens* above it, which means *Willing and Able.* The greeting in the unit in 1974 was "Cotton balers."

According to Army records, the 7th Infantry Regiment has fought in more campaigns than any other Infantry regiment in our Army, having fought in twelve wars, been awarded seventy-eight campaign steamers, and fourteen unit decorations. It is one of the five oldest continuously serving Infantry regiments in the U.S. Army. It was an honor for DeVos to join the ranks of those who served under her colors.

Ed's first assignment in the battalion was as the assistant S-3, a job familiar to him from his 2-509 Airborne Infantry days. This assignment was typical for most new captains as they joined an infantry battalion as it gives the battalion and brigade commanders a chance to size up the new guy up to help determine if they should trust him to command a rifle company at some later date.

With this understanding, the captain put his nose to the grindstone, knowing if he proved himself, the opportunity to command a rifle company would come in time. After four months of updating the battalion SOP (Standing Operating Procedures), operating the battalion TOC (Tactical Operations Center) when the unit went to the field, and overseeing a host of other tasks, he was selected to command Company B, 3rd Battalion, 7th Infantry Regiment.

* * * * *

Company B, or Bravo Company, was not much different than most other rifle companies in the U.S. Army in April 1974. While the authorized strength of the unit was one hundred and fifty men, only one hundred and twenty to one hundred and thirty soldiers filled the ranks. First Sergeant (1st SGT) Fletcher, a seasoned professional, was the "Top" sergeant. He was good and Ed was blessed to serve with him the entire time he commanded Bravo Company. There were three lieutenants in the unit; the most experienced had graduated from IOBC six months earlier. He was the company XO. The other two lieutenants had graduated from IOBC three months earlier. None of the officers or NCOs wore a Ranger tab and only a few of the NCOs were Airborne qualified. All three platoon sergeants were Vietnam veterans with CIBs. Two of the three were good; the other not so. For the most part, the squad leaders appeared to be ready to go to work, although one-third were older and on their last legs, looking forward to retirement in the next few years. About half of the soldiers in the lower ranks had served in Vietnam and were doing just the bare minimum to make it to the day they could leave the service. Their basic attitude was, "What are you going to do? Send me to Vietnam?" The rest of the unit was made up of younger men who had volunteered to join the Army under the VOLAR program. Several had a year or two of college; most did not. For most of them, Infantry was their first choice as they were looking for a challenge. The unit was made up of men of every color and race and background. It was the typical infantry company in the early days of the transition to an all-volunteer force.

The PT run on the day after the change of command was quite revealing. It was clear to DeVos from the start and confirmed by 1st SGT Fletcher that the more time the company could spend in the field, the better off it would be because that would challenge the newer soldiers and keep the older ones engaged and away from trouble. With that in mind, Ed began to take the unit to the field every chance he could, with emphasis on road marches and two and three day field exercises as soon as they could be arranged. While this training helped, discipline in Bravo Company was like the other companies in the battalion. Over time, those issues became less and less of a problem, although they never were completely eliminated.

DeVos knew it was far better to be tough as nails when taking over a command rather than being a "nice" guy, because if a commander starts off hard, he can always back down some as the soldiers grew to understand his expectations. To do the reverse of that—start easy and then get tougher—almost never works. Ed was not shy about using the tools given to him by the Uniform Code of Military Justice (UCMJ) which gave him, as a company commander, the ability to reduce some soldiers in rank, take some of their pay from them, and/or cause them to be put on restriction and extra duty. He could render a punishment, but then suspend it, thereby holding the judgment over the head of the soldier in question for up to sixty days.

Ed learned a major lesson as he exercised his duties as judge and jury accorded him through the UCMJ to administer justice. He learned the hard way that there are always two sides to every story. Listening to only one side is not true justice. It also pays big dividends to ask the right questions before rendering a proper and fair ruling. To learn this lesson early in his time as the Bravo Company Commander was a lesson he applied to a number of issues from that day on. *"There are always two sides to every story."*

He also noted that several soldiers regularly went on "sick call" first thing in the morning but were then returned to duty several hours later after seeing the medical personnel. With that in mind, one day Ed announced that for those who fell into that category, since they missed the unit's regular PT formation, he would lead a special make-up PT formation the next Saturday morning. After just one Saturday, when the five or six soldiers in question completed their two mile run in *gas masks*, the word spread quickly throughout the unit and DeVos never had to deal with that issue again.

Several months into his command, DeVos stood in front of a board of officers who were recommending that one of his Staff Sergeants (SSG) be released from the Army for being overweight based on a new DA regulation. Ed recommended that the board reconsider this man's situation because this NCO had served his country honorably for over eighteen years, two of which were as an infantryman in Vietnam. Upon further reflection, this board gave this NCO six months to get his weight down to acceptable limits, which this soldier did, thereby ensuring that he could retire with twenty years in the service.

On another occasion, Ed felt his unit was getting a 'raw' deal one weekend when the battalion S-3 gave Bravo Company a funeral detail mission when it was a sister company's responsibility. This led to a rather *heated discussion* between DeVos and the S-3, a somewhat pompous major, which led to the discussion being continued in the battalion commander's office. There the issue was settled by the battalion commander as he agreed with the Bravo Company Commander's position.

Days like those helped the Bravo Company NCOs have a spring in their step and increased pride in their unit. But not all went well for some. Late one Saturday night, Ed was called to go to the Post Stockade to vouch for one of his lieutenants. The officer in question and his wife had gotten drunk at some watering hole in Columbus, and as they were driving back toward post on Victory Drive, the main four lane road leading back to Fort Benning, these two decided to abscond with one of the U.S. flags that was flying in the center of the boulevard to honor fallen soldiers. The Columbus police witnessed this theft and promptly arrested them. Within two or three days, this lieutenant was no longer a member of Bravo Company. DeVos has no recollection of what happened to this individual or his wife.

* * * * *

The 3-7 Infantry battalion commander for the majority of the time Ed commanded Bravo Company was LTC Dick Gillem. A soldier from a long line of soldiers; his great grandfather was a general in the Union Army during the Civil War and his father served in World War I and II. Fort Gillem near Atlanta is named for the battalion commander's father, Lieutenant General (LTG) Alvin Gillem. Dick Gillem was a good battalion commander. Having served in Vietnam in a Pathfinder unit in the 1st Cavalry Division, he knew his way around soldiers, and as such, he gave his four company commanders, all of whom had served in combat in Vietnam, appropriate guidance and then gave them some maneuver room as they implemented his guidance.

In Ed's case, this meant he began to focus on the last one hundred yards by taking his men to the rifle range as often as he could, melding those times into other training opportunities such as 'Guidon Runs' back to the unit area. The guidon is a small flag that sits atop a pole that designates company-size units. These runs were quite simple. The unit would run back to the company area as individuals whenever the company commander decided. It might be five miles away from the unit area or it could be longer. Whoever made it to the company area with, or in front of DeVos who carried the unit colors, would have the rest of the day off. Those who finished the run behind the guidon would carry on with their regular duties for the remainder of the day. Motivated soldiers love incentives like this.

* * * * *

The largest exercise 3-7 Infantry took part in while DeVos commanded Bravo Company was held at Fort Stewart, Georgia, southwest of Savannah in November 1974. The bulk of the battalion deployed by C-130 early one morning to maneuver against some armored units of the 24th Infantry Division. Once on the ground, as Bravo Company was getting into position to do great damage to the opposing unit, the twenty-seven year old captain received a radio call telling him there was a helicopter in-bound to his location to take him back to Fort Benning. Susan was about to give birth to their second child.

While this was not a surprise, unbeknownst to DeVos as he was winging his way to Fort Stewart, his mother who was visiting in case the expected baby came while he was deployed, was driving Susan to the hospital and it took a while for the word to reach him. The ride back to Fort Benning in an OH-58, a light observation helicopter, took several hours, arriving late in the afternoon. Since the mother and baby were at Martin Army Hospital, it seemed only right that the pilot, Ted Burell, land the bird on the hospital pad which raised some alarms since he hadn't been given clearance by flight operations to do that. Nevertheless, into the hospital goes Ed with his .45 cal pistol on his hip and camouflage all over his face and hands, looking for his wife and newborn son. Barring his path into the Maternity Ward was 'Nurse Ratchet,' who told him that "Yes" his wife and son were doing fine, but he could go no further with a gun. After a short discussion, they reached a compromise. The captain surrendered his weapon to the nurse for safekeeping and he went to see his wife and Keith Aaron DeVos. It was a great day.

After a day or two, making sure everyone was OK on the home front, Ed caught a helicopter ride back to Fort Stewart in time to hand out cigars and congratulate his XO for doing a great job, grateful for the support his mom and dad gave to Susan and his children in this time of need.

* * * * *

On three occasions, Bravo Company was given the opportunity to operate independently from the battalion. The first was a training exercise that took place in Eglin Air Force Base using aviation assets from Fort Rucker, Alabama where the Army trains its helicopter pilots. For a week, Captain DeVos had on-call fifteen helicopters flown by pilots in training to move his company day or night around a rather large piece of Eglin to conduct maneuvers of his choice. It was a thrill to have so many aviation assets at his beck and call and to conduct any exercise he desired.

The second time the company was off by itself was to deploy to the Panama Canal Zone for intensive jungle training which, in 1974, was called the Jungle Operations Training Course (JOTC). The training there was supervised by an experienced cadre of jungle experts skilled in jungle survival skills, land navigation and movement through very dense terrain, and infantry tactics unique to that severe environment. It was a great time for DeVos to be with his soldiers away from the flagpole.

Ed never learned nor did he ask why Bravo Company was selected for this deployment or the earlier training exercise at Eglin, but he was grateful for the experience. Fifteen years later, he would return to JOTC when he commanded a battalion. The snakes were larger and monkeys were louder that second time around. JOTC has since been moved to the island of Oahu, Hawaii.

The third time Bravo Company was detached from its battalion was on 14 June 1975 when the U.S. Army celebrated its 200th Birthday. This date is also known as Flag Day. Because of the auspiciousness of this event, Fort Benning went all out to make it a great day of celebration. President Gerald Ford, our country's thirty-eighth president (who, according to Ed's mother, was a high school classmate of hers in Grand Rapids, Michigan) accepted an invitation to be present for the ceremonies which included a Pass in Review on the parade field in front of Infantry Hall. Five companies of soldiers stationed at Fort Benning were selected to pass in review that day. Bravo Company, 3rd Battalion of the 7th Infantry was one of those five.

It was a beautiful warm summer day. A soft breeze from out of the west was sufficient to gently blow all the flags and unit colors on display. Temporary bleachers had been erected around the enormous parade field as an estimated thirty thousand people filled every seat. Bravo Company looked sharp that day, buoyed by the cheers of the crowd and the salute given the unit by the President as the company passed by him in review. All of the men in the unit were proud to be a part of that day, knowing it was one of the occasions they could tell their children and their grandchildren about. It was and still is a day to remember.

When Bravo Company returned to the unit area, 1st SGT Fletcher had a large keg of cold beer waiting. The soldiers appreciated the gesture and in short order, most of the men, including their company command-er, were telling stories and sharing about what they had experienced to-gether in Fort Stewart, at Eglin, and in Panama. No one was feeling any pain as the excitement of the ceremony combined with the warm sunshine and the cold beer. After a bit of recovery time to get his head on straight, Ed made it home, but he was in no shape to attend the gala dress blue uniform celebration that was held later that night.

* * * * *

Two months later, DeVos' command of Bravo Company came to an end. It was a bittersweet day but it was time for another man to have an opportunity to lead these infantry soldiers. Those seventeen months in command as caretaker of Bravo Company had gone by quickly, too quickly. In looking back on those days, Ed felt he had done a reasonable job, but felt he could have done better, much better. As he played back many of those days in his mind, he began to recognize missed oppor-tunities. He wasted time on some days when he could have been more efficient. He realized that, if he had spent more time training his subor-dinate leaders, they, in turn, could have passed on more knowledge and skills to those under them that much quicker. While his leadership style was effective, he gave himself an overall grade of 'B.' Little did he know then that there would be opportunities in the years ahead for him to make up for these shortcomings.

A day or so before the change of command ceremony took place, Ed was told he would not be assigned to another position in the 197th Infantry Brigade just yet because his name had been submitted to Post Headquarters as one of those to be interviewed to be the Aide-de-Camp for the new commanding general of Fort Benning who was to arrive in a few weeks.

* * * * *

Before going any further, the reader will note that God has not been mentioned since the first chapter. That is because, while knowing God was important to the DeVos', there were many times when He was put on the back burner. While Ed and Susan attended the local Catholic churches frequently wherever they were stationed, there was no true personal relationship with their Heavenly Father. Both of them, from time-to-time, felt this longing to get closer to God, but because things were going pretty well for Ed's military career, neither stepped out too much to look for a deeper relationship with God. Yet, they knew there was something missing in their lives, a void that needed filling.

One afternoon Susan spoke with the priest at the Catholic Church the family had been attending. This man gave her some precious guidance, essentially saying that she should worship where she felt God was leading her. If that was not in the Catholic Church, she should look at other places of worship to discover which would be best for her in order to have a deeper relationship with God.

When Susan and Ed first started going together in their teenage years, she had attended several services in the Methodist church where the DeVos' were members and understood some of the differences between the two denominations. Now, with the blessing of this priest, both she and Ed felt they could look at the Protestant faith in a new light. This began a journey that continues to this day as Jesus Christ has become the center of their lives. As this story progresses, you will see a transformation in both of their lives.

* * * * *

Ed was the Aide to Major General (MG) Willard Latham from August 1975 through mid-July 1976. It was an assignment unlike any he had experienced before. General Latham was a short, stocky man of great intellect and purpose, and from DeVos' perspective, he came to Fort Benning knowing what he needed to do and was laser focused on driving toward the goal of moving Fort Benning forward.

On his first day, General Latham sent out a one-page memorandum to all commanders, leaders, and supervisors on the post entitled *Leadership at Fort Benning*. In all the time that Ed worked for this man, he never saw him deviate from modeling his core values expressed in that memorandum which stated: (1) Leaders were expected to be totally involved in their unit. (2) Leaders were expected to be technically and tactically proficient. (3) Leaders were to develop mental toughness in themselves and in their units. (4) Physical Fitness was indispensable. (5) Leaders must demonstrate spiritual soundness. In this one page, this man summarized what he believed and what he expected of others. He said what he meant and meant what he said.

The new aide was also privileged to be around the other members of the Post command group. COL John Henchman was the Chief of Staff and COL Ned Showalter was the deputy chief (both are deceased). These men, like General Latham, were veterans of both Korea and Vietnam. COL Showalter earned the Medal of Honor in Korea and all three men wore Silver Stars. Along with the post CSM, Vincent Rojaries (also deceased), DeVos had a number of great soldiers around him to keep him straight. In addition to these men, the two ladies who were secretaries to the command group had been in their positions for over fifteen years. Their wealth of historical knowledge about Fort Benning was extremely valuable.

For this captain, each day was educational, filled with something new and interesting, whether it was escorting some important foreign or U.S. dignitary, all through the well-coordinated efforts of the Protocol Office, or sitting in the back of some briefing room where important issues were discussed. There were numerous trips to be planned, coordinated, and organized for the meetings that required General Latham's attendance. It was an exciting time as the Army considered new pieces of major war-fighting equipment as well as relooking at war-fighting doctrinal issues needed for the next war. Then there were a host of evening functions, both formal and informal, that found their way onto the CG's schedule several times a week, one in particular that required his aide to change from his fatigues into his dress blues in the back of his VW Beatle. It can be done, just not easily.

Many of the trips Ed took with the CG focused on the new war-fighting equipment under consideration or the doctrine to get the maximum use out of their capabilities. The three major weapons the Infantry School was involved in during this time were the new Mechanized Fighting Vehicle known then as the MICV which became the M3 Bradley Fighting Vehicle, the XM1 known now as the M1 Abrams tank, and the UH60, which in its trial days was called the UTTAS, short for Utility Tactical Transport Aircraft System. The procurement of each of these systems were large dollar decisions for the Army, and despite the complexity of each system, the process seemed slow to DeVos. In retrospect, based on how these systems performed on the battlefields of the 1990s and beyond, it appears that those who labored through this cumbersome decision making process knew what they were doing.

One of the most interesting days Ed had as an aide was when he and the CG flew to Aberdeen Proving Ground (APG) south of Aberdeen, Maryland. There he and the general had the opportunity to compare the proposed new equipment with the Russian vehicles they could meet on some future battlefield. First, they took a ride on one of the all-terrain 'bump course' at APG in a Russian Mechanized Infantry vehicle, a BMP. Then the two men rode over the same course on the MICV. Then they rode on the course a third time, this time in a Russian T-62 main battle tank, before riding on the course a final time in the XM1. Without question, the proposed U.S. Army vehicles were the hands-down winners on every obstacle they traversed that day. DeVos even made the statement to General Latham that he almost felt sorry for the Russians. Not that sorry mind you, but it seemed to him that the Russians' only chance was to have so many vehicles that 'we' would run out of ammunition before 'we' killed them all.

A few months later, a highly anticipated demonstration of the helicopter to replace the UH-1 Huey was held at Fort Benning's Lawson Army Airfield, with the three large aviation companies—Bell, Boeing Vertol, and Sikorsky—all vying to be awarded this large contract. It was quite a spectacle, watching each of these helicopters show off their capabilities with great speed, dexterity, and maneuverability. Watching a helicopter scream down the runway before it executed a 360 degree loop is something Ed will never forget. In 1976, at the end of a very long process, Sikorsky Aircraft Company was awarded the contract. The aircraft known today as the UH-60 Blackhawk came on line in 1979. From then on, whenever DeVos flew in a Blackhawk, he always thought of that bird making a loop at Lawson Field.

Moving along at a somewhat quicker pace were the doctrinal issues associated with the updated philosophies of the Air-Land battle, which required a major rewrite of Field Manual 100-5, Operations (FM 100-5). Both the Infantry School and the Armor School at Fort Knox had different views on some major points that were to be included in the 1976 updated version of this manual. Each school had a number of experienced officers working on these issues, but neither school was willing to give much ground on their long-held beliefs.

With a deadline looming and no real end in sight, DeVos received a phone call one day from the aide to General William DePuy, the Commanding General of Training and Doctrine Command (TRADOC), the headquarters that was above both Fort Benning and Fort Knox. The message was simple. There would be a meeting in two days at Fort Knox.

The only attendees would be General DePuy, General Latham, and General Donn Starry, the CG of Fort Knox. No colonels or others who had been part of the writing project were to attend.

Two days later, DeVos and General Latham flew to Fort Knox. The meeting was held at one of the post's VIP guest houses and no "horse holders," an old Civil War term for aides like DeVos, were to be in the room. For three hours, these three men literally rolled up their sleeves around a dining room table and hammered out the sticky points that their staffs had been haggling over for months. At the end of the meeting, FM 100-5 went to the presses. It was a great lesson that General DePuy modeled that day. "When in charge, take charge."

* * * * *

Like all soldiers who, from time-to-time, have an event that is seared deep into their heart and soul, one of General Latham's memories from the Korean War was seeing soldiers who were not in the best physical condition try to respond to horrific combat situations. Because of that experience, in every unit he later commanded, he made physical conditioning a top priority. Fort Benning was no exception. Every day, late in the afternoon, those around main post would see three men running three, four, or five miles and sometimes longer. These three were the commanding general, the post command sergeant major, and the CG's aide. Under General Latham's watch, he also ordered a monthly post-wide five mile run, usually held on Friday afternoons. Ed was the pace man with every unit on post behind him, totaling twenty-five to thirty thousand men and women, depending on the day.

Late one Friday, after one of these post runs, word got back to General Latham that one chaplain had chosen not to participate because this individual had scheduled a counseling session which conflicted with his participation. A quick investigation verified this information to be true. Although the CG was a religious man, a friend of chaplains, and one who appreciated the role these men of God played in support of the soldiers, the next day, Saturday, DeVos was on the phone to Washington, D.C. to track down the Army Chief of Chaplains. Once found, General Latham and the Chief of Chaplains had a rather short discussion on the phone, the upshot of which was that this chaplain who chose not to participate in the post-wide run was to be reassigned and off Fort Benning not later than the following Monday afternoon. And it was so.

* * * * *

On the personal side, one afternoon when Ed was in the CG's office, the general's secretary came in and said she needed to see the aide *now*—a most unusual event. It turned out that Susan had been alerted that their son, Keith, then a year and a half old, suddenly could not walk. She immediately took him to Martin Army Hospital, where within a short period of time, a team of doctors deemed it necessary to immediately admit this child because he had a serious staph infection in his knee.

Once the CG found out about the situation, the aide was given whatever time he needed to take care of his son. It was a long week for Ed and Susan as they watched this little boy, his legs tied with wrappings to the edge of the hospital bed to keep them from moving, with IVs stuck into his leg. After about a week, the infection cleared up and life returned to normal. The memory of that week would come back to Ed many times over the years that followed as he watched his six-foot-two-inch son score two or three soccer goals in a match, or clear the high bar set at six feet in a track meet, or grab a key rebound in a regional high school basketball game, or launch a golf ball into the air and watch it land two hundred and fifty yards away as it split the middle of the fairway.

* * * * *

As Ed's year as the CG's aide neared its end, Infantry Branch in Washington, D.C. gave him a number of assignments to choose from based on the success he had achieved in his career to that point. He could command a Recruiting detachment; be an advisor to a National Guard or U.S. Army Reserve battalion, or he could be an ROTC instructor. While no specific locations were given him for the first two options, in option three, he had his choice of twenty-two colleges and universities to pick from. After considering all this with Susan, they choose to move to Greenville, South Carolina where Ed would be one of the ROTC instructors at Furman University.

As the days approached for their move to Greenville, there was one final hurdle remaining. It involved Ed's replacement and a helicopter jump into Fryer DZ on the Alabama side of Fort Benning where the CG, the CSM, the aide, and the new aide would jump and then run back to Infantry Hall, a distance of around ten miles give or take a few. If the new guy met that 'PT' test, Ed could be on his way to his new assignment. So, on the appointed day, they jumped into Fryer and DeVos and his replacement made their way back to Infantry Hall, finishing well ahead of the CG and the CSM.

DeVos' last day included a firm shake of the hand with a man he admired. Willard Latham was and still is as of this writing a warrior and a man of principle. Some will always wonder what it was like to be an aide for a general and Ed's answer is always the same. It was helping someone else live their life to the fullest by keeping all the clutter and distractions around them to an absolute minimum, thereby allowing this other individual to give the maximum effort to his job.

* * * * *

As the DeVos' drove away from Fort Benning on that July day in 1976, Susan in one car, Ed in another, making their way gingerly through Atlanta traffic on their way northeast on Interstate 85, he harkened back on what he had learned in the last few years.

First, he knew he always wanted to be around soldiers — Infantry soldiers, the men who lived at the point of the spear. Warriors, who with quiet dignity, sloshed through the mud and the dirt, tripped and fell over logs on the darkest of nights, longing for the challenges to prove that they could accomplish any mission they were given, doing it all with minimal complaints and with a 'Can Do' attitude every step of the way. To serve with such men was an honor and a privilege given to only a select few.

Second, the ROTC assignment would give him an opportunity to instill into the next generation of officers some of his experiences, his beliefs, his desires to serve his country as only few could. He wanted them to learn from his seven years in the Army, four of which were in combat units — Germany, Vietnam, and Fort Benning — what the Army was all about. He wanted to pass on his impressions of the last year, that the Army was moving forward, about the new equipment. of what he had been privileged to hear from briefings in a number of higher headquarters, to include the Pentagon.

Third, in some ways, he was glad he was getting a little older because it meant that he was seeing old friends and others he had served with at various places so they could share stories and encourage each other. Through these friendships, they were beginning to leave a legacy, their footprints on the sands of time with others who served and sacrificed for a high calling. That thought reminded him of his younger days as he watched his father on a construction job eating lunch with his fellow carpenters, all veterans of World War II, as they told stories and laughed together. One of these men had been a Marine on Guadalcanal. Another had piloted an F4U Corsair in the South Pacific. Another had been in the transportation corps in Europe. And then there was my father. A bombardier with forty combat missions, in one of which earned the unit a Presidential Unit Citation. As a young man of sixteen, Ed was not a member of that fraternity of old warriors. At twenty-nine years old, he was now part of that fraternity.

8. FURMAN UNIVERSITY, GREENVILLE, SC. BUILDING A LEGACY

The DeVos' looked forward to their time at Furman and for the three years that they lived in Greenville, SC, they were not disappointed. In the Revolutionary War days, Indians and the early settlers occupied this land in the upper western part of South Carolina for both hunting and farming. In 1831 the city was incorporated. In 1976 when Ed and Susan purchased their home in the southeastern corner of the city, Greenville was well on its way to providing homes and work to the more than five hundred thousand who live in the city and its surrounding areas in 2020, making it the third largest urban area in South Carolina.

Furman University's history is closely linked to Greenville's growth since the Southern Baptist Convention established the school in 1828, with the name Furman Academy and Theological Institution. After many years of ups and downs, the university was stabilized by large grants in the 1920s and 1930s. Long before Ed arrived on campus, the university was firmly established on the northern outskirts of the city, with a student body of over two thousand, and highly regarded staff and faculty.

The ROTC program at Furman, like most other ROTC programs, was divided up into four sections of military instruction -- Military

Science (MS) I through IV. In the 1970s at Furman, military science was a mandatory subject for all male freshmen and sophomores and voluntary for females. LTC Art O'Leary, a highly qualified history teacher, taught U.S. Military History to all the freshmen MSI classes and because his classes were so highly regarded, he attracted a number of female students. Captain Mike Pasquarett, a Field Artillery Officer by trade but one who was well-versed in his subject, taught National Security classes to the sophomore MSII students which were well-received by the entire student body.

In addition to his instruction, a major part of Mike's job was to identify and recruit those students he felt had potential to be commissioned through Furman's ROTC program, the primary reason for ROTC units to be on this college campus. Mike's goal each year was to have twenty-five juniors sign papers agreeing to take the next step toward receiving a commission in the U.S. Army. As part of their contract, those who signed on the dotted line received a stipend of one hundred dollars a month. It should be noted that Mike always met or exceeded his goal for the three years he was at Furman.

DeVos' job was then to take these college juniors, called MSIIIs, and prepare them to attend Summer Camp at Fort Bragg, following the same path he had gone through eight years earlier. Upon their return from summer camp, these rising seniors (MSIVs) would then receive instruction from the fourth man on the team, Major Fred Lamm, a Chemical officer, who would then provide instruction on what these second lieutenants to-be would need once they were commissioned and came on active duty.

Leading these instructors by providing sage counsel as well as helping students and the ROTC cadre navigate through the university protocols and academic hurdles was the Professor of Military Science (PMS), LTC Tom Bryan, a not-too-tall Irishman who always had a smile on his face and a personality that could sell ice cream to an Eskimo. He was a wonderful ambassador for the Army on a highly regarded university filled with PHDs of every description, some of whom had little regard for those who wore the military uniforms of their country. Helping this program along behind the scenes was the president of the university, Dr. John Johns, who had received his college degree from Furman after having been a decorated B-24 pilot in the European Theater in World War II. There was also a sergeant major to keep everyone straight, a supply sergeant, and a secretary. Overall, a great team of people.

* * * * *

Once getting settled into their new home in a fairly new subdivision which included community tennis courts and a large pool around the social area, and receiving their household goods, Ed began his first days at Furman, knowing that things would be different from commanding a rifle company and being in the high-rent section of Infantry Hall for the last year. His first meeting with LTC Bryan was not quite what he expected, but in retrospect, it was exactly what this hard charging Infantry Officer needed to hear.

From that initial meeting, DeVos understood several very important things. First, all of "us" were ambassadors for the Army, and as such, remember that everyone who sees "us" will form some opinion about the Army. Second, while Ed's job was to prepare the MSIII cadets for summer camp at Fort Bragg, which was nine months away, he was to keep in mind that these cadets were not in the Army. They were college students. Therefore, rather than requiring them to have "high and tight" haircuts on this college campus, as LTC Bryan put it, his rule, which he stated with a smile, was that "Cadets must have hair." Third, while there was ROTC drill and ceremonies as well as other formations once a week, he wanted each of his cadre to wear civilian clothes on one of the other days of the week. The purpose of this decree was so the university staff and professors as well as the students could see that these Army guys were not painted green inside and out and they did own other clothes besides their uniforms. Tom Bryan was a master at public relations.

* * * * *

Armed with this guidance, DeVos went to work developing plans to have the Furman MSIIIs excel at the summer camp at Fort Bragg. To him, it was simple. His job was to help these men and women understand that the better they did at Fort Bragg, the more options they would have regarding which branch they would like to serve in and what type of commission they wanted: Regular, like the West Pointers, or a Reserve commission. Since their opportunities hinged on how well they performed at Fort Bragg, the ball was in their court.

From his first meeting with the twenty-five MSIIIs, that became his "sales pitch." You do well at Bragg and you are in the driver's seat. The questions that whirled through the cadets' minds were, "What do we need to do to achieve that goal? What does it take?"

That is where the captain's training plan came in, which he began to execute little by little so that their confidence was at its peak just before they would go to Fort Bragg. First, he stressed physical fitness training from Day One to give cadets the best chance to lead the way and stay as fresh as possible for whatever challenges came their way. To give his students the best chance to practice the Army PT test, he built the obstacles so they could practice. Second, he wanted them to learn what command presence and military bearing were all about: to give precise commands in front of soldiers; to be sharp in their dress; to have a command voice. Third, he trained them on basic soldier skills such as day and night land navigation, marksmanship, first aid, and simple squad tactics using the thick woods that existed on the campus at that time and on the university's golf course at night. Fourth, to increase their confidence in themselves, he taught them rappelling, putting the cadets off the second floor of the university field house. This activity became so popular, a number of MSI and MSII cadets participated, which also had a positive impact on recruiting. Last, even though it was not something the MSIIIs would see at Fort Bragg, he put all his cadets through the Ranger water survival test in the university's swimming pool. This included the final part of the survival test where the cadets were "guided" individually off the high diving board while blind-folded, each wearing all their equipment and carrying a weapon. Although DeVos was watching each one of them for any signs of panic, all of these men and women passed with flying colors.

While twenty percent of the MSIII cadets were female, they received no special treatment throughout any of this training. In fact, during the rappelling training and the water survival test, it was "ladies first." What self-respecting man couldn't go after the women had already shown him how? Call DeVos sexist if you want, but this was the late 1970s.

The validation of this training came back each year when the ROTC national headquarters published the ratings for all the colleges and universities based on how their cadets fared at the ROTC Summer Camp. Because Furman students were motivated and smart, Furman cadets were in the top ten percent nationwide each year when they were schooled using this approach, testifying to the recruiting, the training, and the overall desire these students carried deep in their bones.

There were, however, some exceptions. As Ed began to assess each cadet in his charge, he noted that a few evidenced some signs that they may not have the *desire* to be a commissioned officer. His criterion was one question he asked himself about each cadet. "Would I want this man or woman to be one of my platoon leaders? Yes or no?" If this answer was not a resounding "Yes," he asked Major Lamm to keep an eye on the individual to see what he thought about the cadet in question.

After a reasonable amount of time for evaluation, these two officers would make a judgment call and then counsel the cadet to see what was going on in his or her brain. It was almost always a matter of *Will*, not *Skill*. The two officers knew they could teach the *Skill* necessary for the individual to succeed, but the real concern was, did the cadet in question have the *Will* to lead men and women to accomplish a military mission. Through evaluations such as these, several cadets were released from the ROTC program, saving themselves and the instructors' valuable time. This included at least one individual who had been awarded a four-year ROTC scholarship.

Tom Bryan retired a year or so after Ed's arrival, and while the new PCS did not have LTC Bryan's personality, he was wise enough to know that, "You don't fix what ain't broken." So, what had been approved under Tom's leadership, continued without much interference from his replacement.

* * * * *

During Ed's first semester at Furman, LTC O'Leary, the man who taught U.S. Military History, developed a serious medical issue and it was determined he would not be able to teach his three sections of American Military History the last six weeks of that semester. Because all the other instructors were fully engaged in their own responsibilities, it fell to DeVos to finish teaching the rest of the semester in O'Leary's place.

In 1976, Furman operated a three semester system — fall, winter, and spring. The fall and spring were traditional — each student took five or six classes and these classes met three times a week from September through early December, and then March through May respectively. The winter semester was non-traditional, running from mid-January through the later part of February. Students typically took three to four classes and each class met every day.

For DeVos, instead of being able to give his full attention to the preparation for the winter and spring semesters to teach his MSIII students, he was now under the gun to learn all he could about World War I, the time between the two World Wars, World War II, Korea, and then Vietnam. Because LTC O'Leary set a high bar for his quality of instruction, and without the advantage of Google, Ed spent five to six hours each day immersed in a number of books, preparing to teach the next day's three sections at 0800, 0900, and 1100. From those books and the notes O'Leary provided, he crammed every night to make sure the quality of instruction presented to these very bright students was the best he could do. Preparing a good outline, rehearsing, and anticipating questions that might be asked became his routine. Based on the feedback he received later, he accomplished the mission. To have this opportunity to substitute for LTC O'Leary proved to be a God-send as this experience broadened his historical knowledge about his profession that most likely would not have been awakened any other way. Ed's passion for the subject continues to this day. It was a true blessing in disguise.

* * * * *

Ed took advantage of the time at Furman to begin the process of obtaining his Master's Degree in Physical Education. Because he did not have a major or a minor in education, he was required to take several evening classes at the undergraduate level in that discipline before he could begin to take Phys Ed courses at the Master's level. Because his tour was going to be only three years long, he knew time would not be on his side, but he took the plunge, taking the required under-graduate courses at night to at least begin to work on his Masters of Phys Ed program. While he ran out of time to accomplish his goal, this provided the impetus to see this goal through to the end at a later date.

During the summer months, Ed went to Fort Bragg for Summer Camp for eight weeks, but he saw little of the Furman students. His responsibility the first year was as the Chief Instructor of Infantry Squad Tactics. A good job for him and he enjoyed it. This position allowed him to walk around through the woods and be with the officers-to-be as they learned from some of the best—NCOs from the 82nd Airborne Division. The next year at Fort Bragg, the summer of 1978, he was privileged to be a TAC officer for one of the Cadet Platoons. It was a good opportunity to compare how other ROTC departments prepared their cadets for Summer Camp versus what Furman cadets had been exposed to. This observation validated that the Furman preparation for ROTC Summer Camp was right where it needed to be.

DeVos also had an opportunity in the fall of his second year at Furman to attend a five-day course entitled, Wilderness Instructor Training Course. Along with fifteen other ROTC instructors from various universities, these men gathered at Seneca Rocks, West Virginia where for two days they climbed some not too tall but very tough cliffs before rappelling back down. It is interesting to note that the 10th Mountain Division trained at Seneca Rocks prior to being deployed to Italy in World War II. The following day they went spelunking, which means they crawled through caves, some quite large and others very narrow and tight, testing each man's level for claustrophobia. Then the final two days they trekked twenty miles through the woods to West Virginia's highest peak, Spruce Knob. All in all, a great experience with a good group of guys.

* * * * *

In the spring of 1979, Ed received orders. He would be leaving Furman and going back to Germany, this time to V Corps Headquarters located near the heart of Frankfurt, a bustling metropolitan city, the financial hub of that country.

As he and Susan pondered these orders, they looked forward to this move with excitement. They felt blessed for having lived in the vibrant city of Greenville for three years. They had enjoyed their home and their neighbors; the weekend bridge parties, the social gatherings at the neighborhood pool, and the playful banter of the rivalries between the various universities represented in their neighborhood—Furman, Wofford, South Carolina, and Clemson. They had been part of a great university, celebrating in some of the great athletic accomplishments as Furman's athletes bested some of the larger universities—North Carolina, North Carolina State, South Carolina, and Clemson—sometimes in football and other times in basketball. They enjoyed sponsoring a group of twenty freshmen students, welcoming them to the campus, encouraging, and helping them adjust to being away from home. Each Thanksgiving the DeVos' opened their home to Furman students who would be away from their families for the holiday, giving them a place to share a meal on this unique American holiday. While Ed would miss his daily runs around the beautiful Furman campus with the university's registrar, Paul Anderson, and the chair of the Philosophy Department, Dr. Tom Buford, he cherished their friendship and their insights during their times together.

One event Susan would not miss was to be in front of the line the day the MSIII cadets received their medical shots before summer camp. In preparation for the family's return to Germany, she and the children came on campus expecting to get their medical shots after the cadets. However, those in charge moved her along with Kristen and Keith to the front of the line. In true Infantry fashion to "Follow Me," they put on brave faces and complied, but not happily.

Ed and Susan knew they would also miss their church—Mitchell Road Presbyterian Church. It had been the center of much of their time and talents while they lived in Greenville. Susan teaching pre-school there, and Ed singing in the choir and teaching Sunday School for several years. Kristen and Keith received good nurturing in their respective classes. Most importantly, the Word of God began to take on new meaning to this family. While the DeVos' were certainly a work in progress, they experienced a closer relationship with God than they had felt before.

They also knew that it would be back to the military's longer hours as their time living a somewhat "normal" life that is so rare for military families was at an end. No more eight to five days. No more expecting Ed home for supper every night. There would be no more going to college basketball games and football games where it was part of ROTC cadres' duty to attend. It was time to get back to the Army. It was time for Ed to have his equipment packed and ready to be deployed in two hours to go meet the Russians in the Fulda Gap. It was time to be ready for the phone to ring at any hour of the day or night, signaling another alert, another world or regional crisis, or another urgent matter to be solved or resolved within the unit.

It was the life Ed and Susan had chosen. Each military unit has a slogan every member of the unit lives by; to inspire them, to encourage them, to unify them, to give them a sense of purpose. Each and every day those who wear the uniform of our country and their families who support them, live the words expressed in these mottos, these slogans, these axioms: Willing and Able...Deeds not Words...Frightened by No Difficulties...To the Top...We will find a way....We shall innovate, lead, and set an example.

It was time for the DeVos' return to that way of life, buttressed by the knowledge that they had helped others grasp the understanding of the words, "Duty, Honor, Country."

* * * * *

As with a number of other careers and occupations, officers and NCOs in the Army never really know the true impact they leave on others as they move from one location to another. There are times during these

moves when the officer or the NCO wonders, "Did I make a difference?"

Ed had taken to heart some of Tom Bryan's first words — "You will
always be on parade." He felt in his gut that he had been part of a team
that had done a pretty good job of planting seeds and ideas into the
heads of some very intelligent young men and women. He was pleased
with how the cadets responded to the team's directions as they met their
goal of receiving a commission as second lieutenants in the U.S. Army,
knowing that each new officer would be an asset to any unit they would
be assigned. The team had instilled *Will* and the *Skill* into each young
officer so they could excel at whatever they sank their teeth into. He was
proud to be member of this team that played a part in the maturation
process of such good men and women.

* * * * *

Almost forty years later, a reunion was held one evening on the Furman
campus to honor the contribution Tom Bryan and those who were on
his team made on their cadets in the late 1970s. Mike Pasquarett, Bill
Mayville, and several others did all the heavy lifting to bring everything
together. Sixty to seventy former Furman ROTC cadets and their spouses attended. In this group was one Lieutenant General (LTG John Mul-
holland — Infantry), two Major Generals (MG Kevin Wendel –Infantry
and MG Richard Longo — Field Artillery) and one Brigadier General
(BG David Estes — Armor), and too many Colonels and Lieutenant
Colonels to count — all men and women who had been cadets during
the time this team of instructors served together. Their expressions of
thanks were heart-felt, sincere, and genuine. It was good to know the
legacy imprinted on these cadets by Tom and those who were part of his
team made its presence felt in Iraq, Afghanistan, and other foreign soils.

9. V CORPS, FRANKFURT, GERMANY.
A PERIOD OF GROWTH

After spending a few weeks on leave with family, the DeVos' flew to Germany in early August 1979, flying to Rhein-Main on the outskirts of Frankfurt, where they were met by Ed's sponsor who had already arranged for housing for them in the largest U.S. military housing area, which also contained the grade school for the children. Large ball fields were nearby. Their three-bedroom space was furnished with temporary furniture until their household goods arrived about a month later. It was a twenty-minute walk through one of Frankfurt's large city parks to the U.S. Army's V Corps Headquarters complex where Ed would be working. Based on Susan's activities, some days she would have their car, and, on other days, Ed would have the vehicle. Regardless, gas rationing remained in effect just as it had been in their first tour in 1970-1971.

Military families deal with Permanent Change of Station (PCS) moves a number of times during their time in the service and the "spin" the parents put on each move has a direct bearing on how their children react to the new location. As Ed and Susan explained to Kristen and Keith, this move was going to be another great adventure. This tour was supposed to be for three years, but as will be explained, the DeVos' were in Germany for one month shy of twenty-four months. While Ed worked some long hours, the family took advantage of every opportunity to explore Europe.

Geographically, Frankfurt is located near the center of what was then West Germany, three hours by car to Holland to the northwest and four hours by car to the Swiss Alps to the south. By using their time wisely, the family was able to spend a weekend in Holland in both the spring of 1980 and 1981, the prime tulip growing season as these beautiful flowers of every color imaginable bloomed in picturesque fields next to more windmills than one could count. It was during these trips that Keith, all of five or six years old, learned to devour the Dutch cheeses and butter, two of his favorite foods to this day. The family spent several nights in this land of Ed's forefathers in both the farmhouses and bed and breakfast houses nestled along the seacoast. They made time to visit one of this country's gems, Madurodam, a miniature scale of the Dutch countryside, located near Hague.

There was a weekend trip to the French Alps where Ed's ability to speak German was put to the test as the townspeople in one remote village spoke little English. This venture got easier on the second and third days as the family drove through Switzerland, Liechtenstein, and parts of Austria where they explored the depths of a coal mine. When you add the twenty-plus weekend Volksmarches the family took part in throughout the towns and villages in central Germany, the monthly bridge and dinner parties, the post chapel activities, shopping at the Christmas markets in many of the towns, and the kids' weekend soccer games where Kristen could be seen picking a daisy or two from time-to-time instead of watching the soccer ball come in her direction, or Keith learning to play tee ball, the family did not lack for things to do.

One of the highlights for Susan and Ed was to spend two days in the German Alps in the town of Oberammergau where they attended the 1980 production of *The Passion Play*, a world renowned five-hour event which depicts the life and death of Jesus Christ. This play is performed repeatedly over a period of several months on years that end in zero and it has been performed by those who live in the Oberammergau area since 1634 when the townspeople in those days prayed that God would spare them from the ravages of the bubonic plague.

The DeVos' took these and other times of enjoyment and pleasure when they could, because Ed's duties took their toll as they were both important and stressful.

* * * * *

V Corps was one of the major headquarters of the U.S. Army in Europe. Both its crest and its shoulder patch were shaped like a pentagon. Its motto was "It will be done." During the time that DeVos was with this command, the principle combat units that made up the corps were the 8th Infantry Division, the 3rd Armored Division, and the 11th Armored Cavalry Regiment, each equipped with the M1Abram Tanks and the M3 Bradley Fighting Vehicles, much like the ones Ed had ridden on four years earlier at Aberdeen Proving Ground. Other major elements in the corps' structure were the V Corps Field Artillery Group, the 12th Combat Aviation Brigade, the 130th Engineer Brigade, the 3rd Support Command and a host of other combat support and combat service support units, totaling over sixty thousand soldiers.

In the event of war, three stateside units—the 4th Infantry Division, the 194th Armored Brigade, and the 197th Infantry Brigade from Fort Benning—would be under the operational control (OPCON) of V Corps once they arrived in country. With a reorganization of the U.S. Army that took place in 2013, V Corps Headquarters was deactivated.

In the 1980s, the commanding general of V Corps reported to several other headquarters. For tactical and strategic matters, V Corps was under the command of Central Army Group Headquarters (CENTAG) commanded at that time by a German four star. VII U.S. Corps stationed in Stuttgart, West Germany, II and III German Corps, and the 1st Canadian Division as well as a host of combat support and combat service support units also fell under CENTAG. For U.S. support, V Corps took its orders from U.S. Army Europe (USAREUR) headquarters, a four star headquarters located in Heidelberg, West Germany.

* * * * *

V Corps Headquarters was housed in the I.G. Farben Building, nicknamed "Pentagon Europe" because General Dwight Eisenhower had established his headquarters there for a time right after World War II. This massive complex took three years to build in the 1920s when it was constructed to house the I. G. Farben Company, the world's largest chemical company at that time. Over seven hundred and fifty feet long and nine stories high, it was the largest office building in Europe until 1950. One of the unique features inside the structure was its paternoster, a type of elevator that consists of an open chamber that moves slowly in a loop that never stops. Passengers step on and off this elevator on any floor they like, and while it does take some getting used to, especially when you are carrying a lot of papers and/or briefing charts, the system is very efficient. Today the Farben Building is part of the western campus of the University of Frankfurt.

* * * * *

Ed was one of two men with the title of "Exercise Coordinator" in G3 PLEX; PLEX short for Plans and Exercises, and since G3 was the operational hub of the Corps, anything to do with the plans and exercises came through this office. LTC Ken Lucas was the Chief of G3 PLEX, one of the hardest working men Ed has ever seen. A consummate staff officer, he was precise and unflappable, a calm presence in any storm.

136

Three majors in this office of six men worked exclusively on the Corps General Defense Plans (GDP), updating the many plans and contingencies housed in the secure confines of the PLEX vault. The plans team was also responsible to give all GDP briefings to all senior leaders of the units under the Corps.

Major Jerry Hadley, an experienced tanker, and DeVos were the Corps' coordinators for all the exercises V Corps was involved in, each exercise designed to test and evaluate some aspects of the GDP, looking for "holes" in these plans that required correction or more thought. G3 PLEX occupied a large corner section on the third floor of the Farben Building behind a locked steel door in a high-level classified vault. There was a large briefing room behind the steel door as well. Typical days for this team were from 0700 to 1900 Monday through Thursday and 0600 to 2100 on Fridays. There were some weekends spent in the vault, but thankfully, not that many. Because of the classification of their work, nothing was ever taken home by any member of the team nor will any specifics of what this team was involved with be provided in this paper.

* * * * *

The exercises that Jerry and Ed were involved with took two basic forms: Command Post exercises or CPXs, and Field Training Exercises (FTX). CPXs normally required some movement of unit command posts and communication equipment. They usually took place over a period of several days to a week or more, depending on the goals of the exercise and, on some occasions, were held in large gymnasiums where maps of the vast areas of the V Corps terrain could be spread out on the floor.

As an exercise coordinator, it was Ed's responsibility, under the guidance of Ken Lucas, to coordinate any and all details of the exercises he was personally responsible for with all participating units. This required working backward from what the goals of the exercise were to be and then coordinating all efforts of the entire V Corps staff, from communications to medical support, from engineer requirements to intelligence concerns, from aviation support to public relations, all the transportation requirements, and everything in between. IPRs or In Process Reviews were periodically given to the V Corps senior staff and to all the participating units by Ed and other select members of the corps staff. Almost all of these briefings were held in the G3 PLEX briefing room. The larger the exercise, the more briefings and time were required. As an example of the preparation, while Exercise *Able Archer*, a CPX, was normally held in November, detailed planning for the November 1980 *Able Archer* began in March 1980. Since the corps was involved in other exercises such as *Crested Eagle*, another CPX with different goals than *Able Archer*, to be held in the summer of 1980, planning, preparation, and coordination for these exercises overlapped.

When you put an FTX over that, which involved the movement of tens of thousands of soldiers and their equipment, some deploying from the United States, you have a very busy and demanding environment. A major exercise called REFORGER, short for Return of Forces to Germany, took place every year, alternating from CPX to FTX. In either case, attention to detail and being extremely well organized were some of the requirements it took for the exercise coordinators to keep everything on the straight and narrow.

Much of the coordination for these exercises, both CPXs and FTXs, took place through classified messages which required Ed and Jerry to spend a great deal of time and energy walking the halls of the Farben Building coordinating all the information the V Corps staff needed to pass to other headquarters regarding the various exercises. "Getting a chop" or approval from all the V Corps staff offices involved insuring that what was sent out to the units was correct.

It was a lengthy, detailed, time consuming process, but a necessary one. It insured that all units were literally on the same page. Invariably, once a six or seven page message had been sent, within twelve hours one of the units who had received the highly classified message would call asking about x or y or z. Knowing that the information was in the body of the message, Jerry and Ed's response would always be the same: "Read the message." Since there was always the same one or two units who had trouble reading the entire message before calling G3 PLEX with questions, the two exercise coordinators were a bit more caustic in their response to them, responding with, "Read the blank, blank message."

* * * * *

For REFORGER 1981, code name *Certain Shield,* Ed was the V Corps exercise coordinator. It was an FTX involving all the V Corps units mentioned earlier and the deployment of two state-side divisions: the 1st Cavalry Division and the 4th Infantry Division. Planning for *Certain Shield* began in detail one year earlier. The myriad of requirements was extremely large: from the coordination of the movement of the 1st Cav across the Atlantic to making sure that German street sweepers were at specific road junctions to clear mud off the roads so civilian vehicles could travel safely after the passage of large tank formations, and everything in between.

Because of the involvement of these major stateside units in *Certain Shield,* DeVos was dispatched to brief the general officers at Forces Command Headquarters (FORSCOM) based in Atlanta, Georgia. For this particular briefing, Ed, the only V Corps representative, needed to be on his game. All the slides were in the right order; he was well rehearsed and was prepared for whatever might come his way until...two minutes before the briefing was to begin to the four star and his staff of three, two, and one stars...the small little pin fell out of the frame of his glasses, causing the glasses to fall apart. As he reached down to find that little pin, he ripped the backside of his trousers. Now, he couldn't see his charts and briefing slides very well and he certainly couldn't turn his back to his audience, and it was time to start the briefing. It was a good thing he had his act together.

Perhaps the best way to think about the role of the exercise coordinator is to think about him as the drum major of a very large band, charged with getting everyone in step and marching to the same beat in a very long parade stretching out over many miles. All the months of preparation, briefings, meetings, rehearsals, and practices are forgotten when the band performs magnificently during the parade. Each exercise took a monumental effort by a great number of people, some who were more visible than others, to achieve the intended goals. Exercise coordinators received much of the praise when each exercise accomplished its intended purpose but the contributions of many others cannot be overstated. Each exercise was a team effort.

* * * * *

The exercise coordinators also had other responsibilities on the plans side of G3 PLEX. Alerts were a way of life in the 1970s and 80s in Germany. There were CENTAG alerts, USAREUR alerts, and NATO alerts, all of these coming without warning, day or night, any day of the week. When the phone calls came, nothing else mattered. Everyone dropped what they were doing and headed to their war-time location. No one knew when an alert was called if it was a test or if the Russians or another country were showing signs of trouble.

DeVos' wartime mission was to be one of the operations officers in the V Corps Tactical Command Post (TAC CP). The TAC was a small group of vehicles with state-of-the-art communications equipment that would be well forward, relatively close to the expected battle, to be able to provide real-time information back to the V Corps Main Command Post. When the "whistle blew," Ed and Jerry Hadley and a small group of other officers and NCOs needed to be rolling in their three tracked vehicles toward their initial war-time location within two hours of notification, regardless of the day or the time of the alert. This drill was rehearsed many times. During one alert, Ed and Jerry set the TAC up inside a barn right next to a small out-of-the-way German village. To have the town bakery, pronounced *backerei*, just down the street was a real treat. Sleeping on some straw next to the cows that night wasn't too bad either. Sometimes you just have to make do.

As part of the plans team, DeVos also attended a number of meetings at CENTAG and USAREUR headquarters to iron out various issues in the overall GDP of Europe. He also spent some time at the British Forces headquarters in Bielefeld, West Germany. It was quite an education to see how their officers went about their business.

* * * * *

In March 1980, Ed was promoted to major. It was a large ceremony held in the G3 PLEX conference room. As he went back into his office, his phone rang. Having answered calls for years with "Captain DeVos," he was suddenly dumbstruck. The words "Major DeVos" were just simply too hard to say at that moment because, at thirty-two years old, he had been a captain for over one-fourth of his life. But he soon got over it.

A year later, in March 1981, Ed was given a choice, one that would change his career for the rest of his days in the Army. For months, Ed knew his name had been batted about for him to be reassigned to an infantry unit somewhere in V Corps. Because of all the briefings he had given to senior leaders throughout this command, he was well known and if asked, he always said he wanted to get back to soldiers as soon as possible. He also knew he had been selected to attend Command and General Staff College (CGSC) at Fort Leavenworth, Kansas, this selection meaning he was in the top half of his contemporaries.

One morning he was told that the V Corps G1, the colonel responsible for all personnel issues in the corps, wanted to see him. After re-
porting to this man, the colonel told Ed two things. First, V Corp had
received a specific request from the CG of the 8th Infantry Division for
DeVos to be reassigned to be the XO of a mechanized infantry battalion
at Lee Barracks in Mainz. This was the same location, the same buildings, where he had served when he was in 2-509 Airborne Infantry as
a lieutenant. LTG Scott, the V Corps CG, had already approved this
transfer if Ed wanted it. Second, the colonel told Ed that, if he wished,
he could attend the July 1981 CGSC class, one year early. If Ed took the
assignment to Mainz, he would attend CGSC in July 1982 as scheduled.
The choice was his.

The colonel went on to say that before Ed made a decision, this man,
who had served at the Military Personal Center (MILPERCEN) for a
number of years and knew how the system worked, wanted to give this
young major some advice. This older gray-headed man went on to say
that if Ed took the Mainz battalion XO position and attended CGSC as
scheduled, in all likelihood after that, Infantry Branch would assign him
to the Army staff at the Pentagon, thereby reducing his chances to ever
be with soldiers after that.

The colonel followed that up with another thought. He said that if
Ed decided to attend CGSC early, Infantry Branch would almost be
certain to assign him to a stateside division after graduation from CGSC
where the chances for him to be with soldiers for a longer period of time
would be greatly increased. It was Ed's decision and he was to let the
colonel know his desires the next day.

Still in a daze, and after getting Ken Lucas' thoughts, which seemed
to mirror the G1's comments, he and Susan discussed their options that
evening. While the Mainz was a "bird in the hand," having the possibil-
ity of being with soldiers for a longer period of time was very attractive.
Going to CGSC a year early and going home that much earlier was also

a real plus. Weighing into this discussion was that this counsel came from a man who had spoken few words to DeVos over the years but who had observed him and seemed to have his best interests in mind.

The more Ed and Susan talked, the more excited they became. While this meant a mad-dash to pack-out their household goods, leaving the family with bare bones quarters for over a month, the adjustments to these inconveniences were worth it in the end. G3 PLEX responsibilities were transferred to others and on the appointed day the family flew back to the States, taking three weeks leave before driving to Fort Leavenworth.

* * * * *

There was no question in Ed's mind that his time as an aide at Fort Benning provided a good foundation to work at V Corps as he was comfortable in front of senior officers. His work ethic was such that he did his absolute best in every task he was assigned and also on those that weren't necessarily his as well. The thought that kept ringing through his head was "Always do your best, no matter the task."

Another lesson that served him well in those days with so much going on around him at such a fevered pace was the value of maintaining a daily "To Do" list. He formed this habit in his first days at G3 PLEX and that still continues to this day. Even if the list is twenty things long, it helps him establish the priorities that govern his day. It is easy to forget things in a busy day and so the list is a living, breathing ever-changing, ever-present reminder of what needs to be accomplished.

Ed felt good about his time at V Corps. He grew as an officer, a father, and as a husband. It was a good two years.

10. FORT LEAVENWORTH, KANSAS.
MISSION ACCOMPLISHED.

After some well-earned leave time, the DeVos's drive from Florida through parts of Tennessee, Kentucky, and Missouri to Kansas opened up their eyes about the size of the United States. Like their previous moves, this was part of the adventure of a military family. Fort Leavenworth is located twenty-five miles northwest of Kansas City, Kansas which sits right next to its larger sister city, Kansas City, Missouri. The fort, named for Colonel Henry Leavenworth, a veteran of the War of 1812 and expeditions against the Great Plains Indians, borders the northern edge of the town of Leavenworth, Kansas, the two linked arm and arm in their history.

Fort Leavenworth is the oldest active United States Army post west of Washington, D.C. and it is the oldest settlement in the state of Kansas with its beginning in 1827. As the country expanded westward, the town of Leavenworth was founded in 1854. In the years that followed, Fort Leavenworth became known as the intellectual center of the Army when the School for the Application of Infantry and Cavalry was founded in 1881. As doctrine evolved, along with practical experience, the school's name was changed to the Command and General Staff College (CGSC). Today, its mission is to educate and develop selected officers to lead our armed forces in the full spectrum of joint and multinational operations.

Fort Leavenworth is also home to the United States Disciplinary Barracks, the Department of Defense's only maximum-security prison. Adjacent to the south side of Fort Leavenworth is a United States Penitentiary which houses over eighteen hundred prisoners in this medium security prison. It is not uncommon to hear the whistles and other sounds coming from this facility in the nearby military housing areas of the fort.

The DeVos' arrived at Fort Leavenworth in mid-July 1981. Ed was one of twelve hundred men and women who would attend the 1981-1982 CGSC class. Within that student body were nine hundred U.S. Army majors and another eighty officers from a combination of the U.S. Air Force, Navy, Marines, and Coast Guard. Added to these numbers were one hundred and sixty foreign officers from Spain, Ghana, Portugal, Great Britain, Canada, Israel, West Germany, France, Holland, Thailand, Japan, Saudi Arabia, and India, to name just a few. All these families, with few exceptions, occupied military housing on the post that was set aside exclusively for CGSC students.

Because the permanent party at Fort Leavenworth goes through the process of welcoming a new CGSC class ever year, the organization for getting these students and their families integrated into the post activities is smooth and, for the most part, hassle free.

The 1981-1982 CGSC student body was divided into twenty large classrooms, with sixty-four officers in each room, all located in Bell Hall. Members in each classroom were then further divided into four sections of sixteen officers, called work groups. To cross-level the experience and knowledge that abounded in the class, the make-up of each work group was some combination of one infantry, artillery, and armor officer and then ten other U.S. Army officers from the air defense, aviation, signal, engineer, quartermaster, medical service, judge advocate's general corps, intelligence, ordinance, military police, chemical, chaplain, and transportation branches. Added to this mix was one Air Force, Navy, Marine, or Coast Guard officer along with two foreign officers. In Ed's work group, the two foreign officers were one from Spain and one from Ghana. An Air Force fighter pilot was also a member of this work group. Most problem-solving exercises held throughout the first half of the course were completed in these work group teams.

While all the students wore their military uniforms, a thread of a college atmosphere was apparent as the normal classroom hours were from 0800 to 1400 Monday through Thursdays and then from 0800 to 1200 on Fridays, giving each officer ample time to pursue other activities and interests, all adding to the maxim that this year at CGSC would be "the best year of your life."

The post was designed to help these student officers enjoy a good family atmosphere. The schools for the children who lived on post, each with excellent ratings, were close to the clusters of student housing quarters and there were many large fields available for playing ball, exercising, or just taking a walk or a run. The large post chapel had a number of activities throughout the week for both the CGSC students and their family members and the DeVos' took advantage of those opportunities. There were always a number of impromptu gatherings, both in the housing areas as well as within the work group. It was a good time to catch up with old friends, like the one night Ed and Susan had dinner with Jack Costello and his wife, the man Ed was tied with as the number one cadet in their platoon at ROTC Summer Camp in 1968. Before his retirement from the Army in 2001, Jack, an Air Defense officer, commanded the Army's Space and Missile Command. He passed away in 2010.

Work group socials were always enjoyable, especially the ones in the afternoons when the entire work group headed for the golf course, giving the officer from Ghana an opportunity, for the first time in his life, to swing a golf club. This was just another way to bring these foreign officers and their families into the fold. They, too, shared with the class their traditions as on Wednesday afternoons through the nine-month course, each country representative and his family entertained the class with something about their culture. Sometimes these presentations featured food, other times dress and culture, other times history. Regardless of their individual styles, it was always enjoyable to learn more about these countries and to support these officers and their families who had traveled long distances to be with their U.S. brothers in arms.

While most countries supported their officers quite well, that was not always the case. Halfway through the CGCS class year, the officer from Ghana was notified through his embassy that he would no longer be welcomed back into his country. A change in Ghana's leadership declared him and his family persona non grata. This man then immediately applied for asylum in the United States, remaining in the Leavenworth area after graduation from CGSC.

For Ed, with so much free time on his hands, he was able to jump into both some new things as well as some old ones. On the new side, he helped coach Keith's soccer team in both the fall and spring. In the winter months, he refereed basketball games in both the CGSC league and the youth programs, giving him a new perspective of this sport as he learned it was a lot easier to ref a game from the sidelines than it was to step forward and grab a whistle. The class schedule also gave him time to pick up his golf clubs again after a two-year hiatus from the game. With time to practice, he got his handicap into the single digits which he parleyed into winning the CGSC Championship in the spring of 1982. It was not an easy win as he choked a bit in the middle of the second round. But in the last few holes, he got his act together and pulled out a one stroke victory. The prize was a new set of woods which he sent to his dad as a gift.

* * * * *

The Command and General Staff College in 1981-1982 had two main thrusts. The fall "semester" concentrated on the theory of war; specifically, when should the U.S. go to war? What were the "national interests" of the United States? What events should or would trigger military action, and how do you define "appropriate" military responses?

Questions like these were discussed at great lengths for several reasons. First, because of our experience in Vietnam, what did "we" as a nation and as professional soldiers learn from that experience? And based on that experience, how should "we" structure our Armed Forces for future conflicts? Second, as the class members were given more responsibilities in their future assignments, how could "we" best advise our political bosses on these issues that our nation might face, who in most cases, would not have never participated in discussions like these.

With such broad topics, there were many ways to break these questions into bite-size pieces which paved the way for lengthy discussions of the pluses and minuses of the various courses of actions that might be considered, particularly in light of the number of powder kegs spread around the globe, some small, some much larger.

The spring "semester" had a number of electives the students could choose from, but the overriding strategic scenario was a major conflict breaking out with Russia in Europe. Not surprising, these war games focused on the V Corps sector. Work groups dealt with defense plans and contingencies for that area based on various assumptions. Once the instructors learned about Ed's familiarity with the V Corps plans, he found himself in the student position of CINCUSAREUR, which stands for Commander-in-Chief of United States Army Europe, a four- star billet. This really didn't amount to much except to say that the instructors wanted others to gain some understanding of what Ed already knew. It was interesting to see how others grappled through these real-life scenarios, comparing their recommendations with the actual plans.

* * * * *

Two major opportunities opened up for DeVos almost as soon as the CGSC year began. First, he now had a chance to get his Master's degree, and second, he became part of an evening study group that a year after he graduated from CGSC became known as the SAMS course, the School of Advanced Military Studies.

During the CGSC year, those officers who had the desire could apply to earn a Master's degree through a program titled the Masters of Military Science (MMAS) degree which was sponsored jointly by Fort Leavenworth and the University of Kansas. To obtain this degree, the CGSC student would work with the CGSC faculty to determine a military subject that needed additional study and would be of interest to the Army as a whole. Agreement between the faculty and the student on the research subject was required by both parties by early September 1981. The thesis had to be turned in by 1 April 1982 to give the faculty sufficient time to judge the work to be worthy of a MMAS degree before graduation from CGSC two months later. Early in the process, Ed knew the title of his thesis: *The Tactical Evolution of the Offensive Chemical Weapons in World War I.* To the civilian world, this subject would put most of them to sleep. To those in the U.S. Army, this subject would raise some eyebrows.

The genesis of this topic was formed in DeVos' head over the years by the constant requirement that in all the units he had been in, except Vietnam, every soldier always had to have his gas mask close at hand in case of an enemy gas attack. Measures to defend against a gas attack were stressed but there seemed to be no thought given to the offensive side of this equation.

Ed knew from his World War I history studies at Furman that every nation — Germany, Great Britain, Russia, France, the United States, and others — had successfully employed gas in the offense. At first, these gas attacks were simple, dependent on shifting weather conditions. But with time and experience, these combatants developed more effective ways to employ gas to help them win on the battlefield. Whenever Ed asked any senior officer, "Why don't we use gas?" he was met with a stare that communicated that "we" would never do that, even though our country has that capability, and our most dangerous foe gave us every indication he would not hesitate to employ these weapons.

DeVos kept asking himself, "Why are we playing this game with one arm tied behind our back? Why shouldn't we at least consider how to employ gas, so the other guy has to take defensive preparations just like they force us to?" Incredibly, not even the Chemical Corps, one of the branches of our Army, seemed to have given much thought to this subject (at least in public forums), choosing instead to put much of its energy on how to use nuclear weapons. Why not chemical weapons as well?

Once the proposed thesis topic was approved, Ed was off and running, using his early mornings, his lunch times, and many afternoons, to plow through books, newspapers, after-action accounts of World War I battles, and every bit of information available in non-classified sources about chemical weapons of that timeframe. Like many researchers, once he began to really dig into who, what, where, when, how, and why of the subject, there was enough information available that several papers could be written, not just one.

Six months later, after many rewrites on an old "hunt and peck" typewriter at three and four o'clock in the morning, Ed gave his work to a professional typist, trusting she could get everything in order. After another month of proof-reading and adding a few more pieces of knowledge, this infantryman turned in his one-hundred-and-twenty-page thesis to his CGSC faculty advisor. That was a good day, but the better one was graduation day in early June 1982 when his name was called as one of thirty officers who invested their time wisely to be awarded their MMAS degrees. A Masters' Degree — Mission accomplished.

* * * * *

Within the first month of classes, De Vos was encouraged to attend a special seminar one night a week to discuss military theory. Colonel Huba Wass de Czega, a highly decorated infantryman, who had a reputation as an innovative thinker, led these weekly sessions. Each week he would give the seven men in this select group a strategic or tactical problem to mull over as he fired questions at them and debated the subject back and forth. These two-hour discussions stretched the minds of each officer in the room, giving them a broader perspective on some of the weightier issues being discussed by the Army's senior leadership.

One year later, with Colonel (later Brigadier General) Wass de Czega at the helm, the School of Advanced Military Studies (SAMS) became a reality, graduating a class of thirteen officers. Since then, graduates from this course have played vital roles in the development of operational plans in almost all of the Army's higher headquarters. As part of their studies, SAMS graduates now receive an MMAS degree as they remain at Fort Leavenworth for a second year.

* * * * *

As their time at Fort Leavenworth was drawing to a close, Ed and Susan looked back at everything they had been a part of for the last ten months and smiled. They had taken a few days to visit old friends from 2-509 Airborne Infantry days in Minnesota. Kristen and Keith had grown physically and academically. Susan and Kristen enjoyed a family excursion to see the Laura Ingalls Wilder house from *Little House on the Prairie* fame. Ed had the chance to watch Larry Bird and the Boston Celtics play in an NBA basketball game in Kansas City. They had made it through a cold and windy Kansas winter and had heard sirens signaling that tornados were in the area. Like their neighbors in their class, they participated in the "Great Yard Sale," an annual event that drew folks from all around Kansas and Missouri to shop for bargains as many of the CGSC families looked to trim unnecessary items they had accumulated in their previous moves before packing up for the upcoming one.

Ed now had his orders in hand. That old-gray-headed colonel in Frankfurt knew what he was talking about. His next assignment was to the 7th Infantry Division, Fort Ord, California. While Ed and Susan were a bit leery of going to the "left" coast, the officers at Infantry Branch who Ed talked to were quite insistent.

Both Ed and Susan had grown in these ten months. Ed had met his goal of getting his Masters. Even though he stayed busy on a number of fronts, he had a much better feel about how to achieve balance in his life — Career, Family, and God were all in the mix. His time management skills, which heretofore had almost solely been aimed at his career, now took into account God and the family as well. Even though he knew that once they got to Ord, the probability of being with soldiers would be high and the strains on his time would increase with those responsibilities, he was thankful that he now understood the importance of having balance in his life; not just for a season, but for a life-time. It was important to make every minute count when he and Susan would be together. Similarly, every quality moment he could spend with his children was important.

The best lesson DeVos learned at Leavenworth kept repeating itself. Have balance in your life. Make every second count. You get no days off from being the best husband and father you can be. They will still be your family long after your Army career comes to a close. Keep the main thing the main thing.

11. FORT ORD, CALIFORNIA.
THE FIRST TWO YEARS.

The day after graduation from CGSC in June 1982, the movers packed all the household goods and the DeVos' loaded up their two cars and headed toward California. Behind their station wagon, they towed their other car, the twelve-year old VW "bug" they had purchased in Germany in 1970. The drive to Fort Ord took five days. First, they headed for Denver, Colorado before turning north toward Cheyenne, Wyoming. Then it was west through Salt Lake City, across the Great Salt Lake, before dropping into Nevada where Ed gave Keith, now eight-years old, a short lesson on slot machines that were everywhere in the motel in Winnemucca, Nevada. The next day it was back on the road through Reno, then Sacramento, before finally reaching Monterey, California, two hours south of San Francisco right on the Pacific Ocean, just south of Fort Ord, late in the afternoon.

Two family stories are remembered to this day about that trip. First, as they were driving through Wyoming, the howling wind blew numerous large tumbleweeds across the highway. After watching this for a time, Susan decided that one of those big bundles of large dried-out plants would be ideal to help decorate their new quarters. So, they stopped the car and stuffed a large bushy tumbleweed into the back of the VW. It remained as part of the house décor for the next four years. Second, once they reached Monterey, dog-tired, they checked into the first motel they could find. But, within five minutes, they checked out as there were more cockroaches in that room than they could count. A second motel, just down the road, was much more to their liking.

* * * * *

In 1917 the land later known as Fort Ord, was established as a field artillery range along Monterey Bay, north of the small town. In 1933, this property was named Camp Ord in honor of Major General Edward Ord, a Union general. After more land was purchased in 1941, it became the home of the 7th Infantry Division and renamed Fort Ord.

The 7th Infantry Division played significant roles in World War I as well as in World War II where it saw action in the Aleutian Islands, Leyte, and Okinawa. During the Korean War, the division took part in the Inchon landing and was one of the units that bore the brunt of the Chinese intervention into that war in late 1950. After hostilities came to an end, its units helped defend the Korean demilitarized zone from 1953 to 1971. When the DeVos' arrived at Ford Ord in June 1982, the division was made up of two infantry brigades and all the combat, combat support, and combat service support units necessary to fight. To the chagrin of many, the post was closed in 1994 as part of the Base Realignment Closure (BRAC) action by Congress.

The day after the family arrived at Monterey, Ed reported into his new boss, the 7th Division G3, LTC (P) John Howard, the (P) meaning he was on the promotion list for Colonel. This energetic officer greeted DeVos with open arms as they had known of each other by reputation because of their service as advisors in Vietnam. Quarters for the family were ready, and in short order, the family was able to move in. Unlike their previous military quarters, this one was a single-family dwelling with a large tree in the middle of their front yard with ice plant on two sides, that tough, hardy succulent that produced beautiful flowers. The house was near the top of a hill which gave them an unobstructed view of Monterey Bay, a mile to the west.

As Susan and the children settled in, Ed got to work as the Chief of G3 Ops for the division, a position he would hold for a little over a year. Along with a team of three officers and seven NCOs, he was responsible for the coordination for almost everything that required the division's use of men and equipment, whether it had to do with operational plans or to run the exercises necessary to train the division to meet its operational requirements. While he had a good understanding of the operational aspects of his position because of his V Corps experience, there was another part of this job that took more time than Ed expected as it involved both military and civilian requests for men and equipment.

Because the 7th Infantry Division was the Army's largest and most important representative in this part of California, the division received many requests for help and/or assistance from a number of civilian organizations and the surrounding cities and towns. While each individual request was, by itself, not overwhelming, there were many occasions, particularly around national holidays, when local towns and cities held parades and other events and they wanted a military presence. While these activities helped build relationships with these communities, each request had to be assessed pitting time, effort, and money against the benefit. Once the decision was made to support an event, then a "tasking" was sent to the subordinate commands to fill the request. Knowing what it was like to meet these requirements at the unit end, DeVos always went the extra mile to make sure all units were treated as fairly as possible.

There was one request that came to his office that every unit in the division stood in line to support. This was the weekend when the "Doolittle Raiders" held their reunion at Fort Ord, the event celebrating

General Jimmy Doolittle's airmen bombing Japan in 1942. Needless to say, all the activities surrounding that event went off without a hitch.

Because Fort Ord was limited in maneuver space, most of the training involving battalion size or larger elements was held sixty miles south at Fort Hunter Liggett or at Camp Roberts, a National Guard reservation, another twenty miles south of Hunter Liggett. While the movement of a division CP was much like the V Corps CP he was acquainted with, one thing surprised Ed during his first division exercise at Hunter Liggett in early July 1982. Late on the first day in the field, DeVos was told he was to eat at the General's mess for his evening meal. As he entered the large tent, he was shocked to see tables were set up with silverware next to each plate. Having always been in units where such opulence would never be considered, this touch of luxury seemed totally inappropriate and unnecessary. The manpower and vehicles to haul around these tables, chairs, and equipment was out of place in a combat unit.

When he quizzed others about this, he was told that the current division commander was comfortable with such surroundings so when the division headquarters went to the field, this was the SOP. Knowing that the division would be changing hands to a new commanding general in the next month, DeVos bit his lip, waiting to see how the new CG would react to such indulgence. When Major General Jim Moore, took command of the 7th Infantry Division, Ed was not disappointed.

* * * * *

General Moore was a soldier's soldier. A second-generation West Pointer, he served his country in infantry command positions in Vietnam, Korea, Germany, as well as in the United States. Because of the responsibilities of his position, Ed was one of the first to brief General Moore on the division's missions, activities, and commitments. It was not unusual for him to brief the CG at least once a week on one thing or the other, always finding him to be attentive and quick to ask questions. In many ways, the man was much like MG Latham, an officer focused on moving his command forward.

As the month's passed, Ed's patience was wearing thin because he was hoping to be with one of the six infantry battalions within his first year at Fort Ord. Sensing this, Colonel Howard counseled the major to be patient. He said more than once, "There are a lot of irons in the fire. Hang in there. It will all work out." Buying into that logic, DeVos kept plowing along, doing the best he knew how to do, no matter what the task. Then the call came.

* * * * *

In early August 1983, DeVos became the S-3 of the 2nd Brigade of the 7th Infantry Division, one step closer to an infantry battalion. The brigade consisted of three infantry battalions: the 1st, 2nd, and 3rd battalions of the 32nd Infantry Regiment. With a staff of ten men, an equal mix of officers and NCOs, he went to work. The Brigade Commander, Colonel Dave Harris, was a calm, level-headed man, with a great deal of experience with soldiers at all levels. LTC Zannie Smith was the Brigade XO. Zannie's first deployment was as a young, enlisted paratrooper into the Dominican Republic with the 82nd Airborne Division in 1965. He became a great friend to Ed over the years as they would be stationed together again later.

DeVos and his crew of men coordinated all the activities of this infantry brigade of twenty-five hundred soldiers. Because he had been in the operations-side of the Army off and on for the last four plus years, he was well-prepared for this position, which allowed him to hit the ground running. First, there was a joint exercise with elements of the Japanese Army, which was then closely followed by a flight to South Korea to coordinate the brigade's involvement in Team Spirit '84 which would be conducted in the spring of that year. Besides these two major events, there were other exercises that kept everyone hopping, such as a large CPX at Fort Lewis, Washington.

Because of his experience in operations, Ed pushed down as many responsibilities as he could to those who worked for him, so they, too, could gain some valuable experience. This paid big dividends when he was tasked to spend several weeks at Fort McCoy, Wisconsin, evaluating a National Guard infantry brigade. Men like Captain Harold Raugh, a man who now holds a PHD, and is, as of this writing, the command historian for the USAEUR, Sergeant Major Chevas, SFC Brent, and others made his job much easier. It was a joy to be around these professionals.

Even though he was good at keeping many balls in the air, on one occasion DeVos almost dropped a big one. In preparation for Team Spirit '84, the largest training exercise in the free world, he and his men put everything together for some preparation drills down at Hunter Liggett, only to have it suddenly dawn on him that this exercise would overlap with Super Bowl weekend. After "eating some crow" in a meeting with Colonel Harris, Ed and his staff hustled and got portable TVs and all the electricity needed so that the soldiers of the Team Spirit task force could see that game. This error would not be repeated by DeVos ever again.

* * * * *

Even though the requirements of his jobs took a great deal of time, Ed and Susan did their best to maintain a balance, spending as much time as possible with their two energetic, growing children. Since their time at Fort Ord turned out to be four years, the family was able to do much more than they ever dreamed of.

Monterey had a number of world–class activities close by: the Aquarium, the Seventeen Mile Drive which ran along on the Pacific

Ocean next to Pebble Beach, and the quaint town of Carmel with its quiet charm and its sand sculpture contests on the beach. There were whale watching cruises off the coast and eating at some of the area's great restaurants which served wonderful, fresh seafood like shark and calamari.

The family took a number of trips: visiting Hearst Castle and some of the smaller towns along the Pacific Coast and a longer trip south to San Diego to go to the San Diego Zoo and to Sea World where Keith was picked out of the crowd to be kissed by a killer whale. As an added bonus, the family stayed near Naval Air Station Miramar, at that time, home of the Navy's Top Gun School. On the way home, the DeVos' stopped in Los Angeles to go to Disney Land Park and Universal Studios.

Some longer trips included a visit to the Grand Canyon, staying in a room next to the rim of the canyon and spending a night in Las Vegas on the way home. Then there was a week in Hawaii at a condo a short distance from the beach on the west side of Oahu. Transportation for this trip was provided by the U.S. Air Force as the family flew Space-A both ways. The flight to Hawaii was in a C-141 Medivac aircraft where everyone had rear looking seats next to the racks where patients were cared for. The flight back was on a KC-135 Tanker where the family sat right behind the flight deck. Cost for each of these flights was about twenty bucks — five dollars per box lunch. The family also took time to take Susan's mom for a short camping trip to Yosemite National Park.

Keith had many firsts: building a fort in the backyard, breaking his wrist while skating; having a run-in with some MPs while policing up brass in the training area close to the housing area; knocking one over the fence for a home run in a Little League game; going to a Christian camp in the mountains south of San Francisco; going to a year-round school; getting pretty good at basketball and soccer. He was all-boy.

Kristen began a growth spurt which, at fifteen when the family moved to our next assignment, almost left her mom and dad breathless: she was growing into being a beautiful young woman. Academically smart, almost too tall for gymnastics, she always had a book in her hand, and she was a bit of a showman as she participated in school plays and musicals. Like her brother, she spent a week in Christian camp near the one Keith attended.

While there were many other remembrances like seeing the 1984 Olympic torch when it came through Fort Ord on its way to Los Angeles, the most significant by far was Susan's introduction to Bible Study Fellowship (BSF) where women of all denominations gathered each week to study God's Word. For her, this was life changing, and it still impacts how the family worships God today. What a blessing. Through the post chapel activities, Ed and Susan began to meet each week with other officers and their wives who were involved in Officer's Christian Fellowship (OCF). With the passage of time, the men and women in that group like Dick Sherwood and his wife, Susie, and Don and Sandy Holzwarth became dear friends. In the years that followed, both of these men retired as Colonels, Dick in the Field Artillery, Don in the Corps of Engineers.

No discussion about trying to maintain balance while stationed at Fort Ord would be complete without a few words about golf, as this part of California has too many great golf courses to count: Pebble Beach, Spyglass, Del Monte, Pacific Grove, and the two Fort Ord golf courses, Bayonet and Black Horse. When he could, Ed would go and maintain some infantry proficiency through golf in the skills of range estimation and terrain analysis. Besides being invited from time-to-time to play with General Moore's golf group, DeVos played in a charity event with members of the 1981 NFL Super Bowl winning Oakland Raiders. His partner that day was Jack Tatum, a two-time All-American at Ohio State, whose nickname in the NFL was "The Assassin." Jack was, and still is, a very, very large man.

Ed was also able to spend some quality time at Pebble Beach. One year he was one of the marshals for the annual pro golf tournament held there. In 1982 when the U.S. Open was played at Pebble, his Father's Day present that year was a ticket for the Saturday round. Then, best of all, when his mother and father visited, Ed and his dad played Pebble Beach on a beautiful sun-filled fall afternoon. Even as his dad got older, he still remembered making a par on the famous eighteenth hole.

* * * * *

Each quarter of the calendar year, all major commands in the division would give the commanding general their "quarterly training brief," laying out their plans for the months ahead. This was a significant event and could take several hours, as each senior commander briefed the CG on their proposed training plan. The bulk of this briefing in an infantry brigade was given by the Brigade S-3.

Soon, after the 2nd Brigade's return from a very successful showing in Team Spirit '84, it was the brigade's time to brief General Moore on the upcoming quarter. DeVos' part of the briefing seemed to go well and there were no major questions or concerns voiced by either the CG or members of his staff. As these officers were leaving the brigade conference room, General Moore looked at Ed and said, "Let's go into your office."

Not sure how badly he had screwed up, all DeVos could say was, "Yes, sir. Right this way." As he led the CG into his office, ready to get his butt handed to him, Ed wondered, "Could it have been that bad? What did I forget?"

As soon as the two men were in the office, the CG closed the door. Without any preamble, he said, "Tomorrow the Lieutenant Colonels' promotion list is coming out. In my opinion, you should have made that list below the zone. But you didn't. I don't know why." He then paused for a moment. "A few years ago I was a Colonel in the Pentagon and my boss came into my office and said, 'The Brigadier Generals' list is coming out tomorrow. You haven't been a colonel for all that long, but I still think you should have made it below the zone. I don't know why they didn't pick you. My advice to you is just keep doing your best and it will all work out.'"

The general then gave Ed a little nod and said, "Here's my message to you. Just keep doing your best and it will all work out." Then he walked out the door.

Dumbstruck, all Ed could do was to stare at the wall. He didn't even know the LTC list was coming out, and he certainly had not given any thought of making that list "below the zone" which meant he would be in the top one or two percent of his contemporaries.

Then his thoughts went in a different direction—General Moore's compassion and understanding. Here was a very busy man with many things to deal with, and yet he took the time to consider that not making a promotion list could be a morale issue for one of his men. He took the time to be an encourager. He took the time to show he cared. This lesson—always be aware of what others might be facing or feeling—was one of the major lessons in Ed's development as a leader.

* * * * *

While it was hard to determine what "Just keep doing your best and it will all work" really meant, the truth of that message came through loud and clear a month or two later when early one morning Colonel Harris told Ed that the CG wanted him to attend a meeting at Fort Leavenworth. Without thinking, DeVos' response was, "Sir, why me? Why can't someone on his staff go to this meeting?"

Dave Harris' answer to those questions was basically, "Major, what part about the Division Commander wants you go to a meeting at Fort

Leavenworth as the division's representative, don't you understand? You are to report to him at 1500 today and he'll give you his guidance. Now get out of here and go pack your bags."

Later that day, DeVos reported to General Moore's office and soon found himself sitting around a small conference table, just the two of them. The CG's comments were short and to the point. "There will be a meeting next week on restructuring several infantry divisions to be smaller, and therefore, more deployable. TRADOC, FORSCOM, and DA action officers will be there as well as a few others to hammer out the TO&E (Table of Organization and Equipment) for these restructured divisions. I want you to go there as my representative. If, during this meeting, you need me, call me on my direct line. Otherwise, use your best judgment. Come see me as soon as you get back. Questions?"

"No, sir."

"Good. Here is a copy of General Wickham's *White Paper 1984: Light Infantry Divisions*. Study it. This should drive your thinking at this meeting. Expect to see some push-back from those who will lose some pride, assets, and prestige in their current missions. Use the CSA's guidance in this paper as your guiding light. I'll see you as soon as you get back."

The translation of this short meeting in DeVos' mind was General Wickham, the Army Chief of Staff, was about to set the Army on a new course with regard to force structure, and like anything new in such a large organization as the United States Army, not everyone will immediately jump on board because these changes may have some impact not to their liking. With regard to any recommendations he might make at this meeting, DeVos' job was to provide the 7th Infantry Division's point of view on any and all subjects. Implied in this was that the division would have some part to play in this restructuring. Without question, the general had not told Ed everything he knew, but the major had enough to get going.

* * * * *

Two days later, DeVos was on a plane to Kansas, reading through the *White Paper1984: Light Infantry Divisions* several times as he jotted down notes, ideas, and thoughts. It was clear from the first reading that General Wickham thought the Army's force structure needed to be more flexible because, at that time, it was skewed toward heavy mechanized and armor forces for a fight in Europe. The CSA's concern was that the Army needed readily available forces for rapid deployment to other crisis areas, not just Europe. By streamlining the size and composition of some infantry divisions, these lighter, more mobile divisions could be rapidly transported by Air Force aircraft to meet threats in multiple locations around the globe. In the *White Paper*, General Wickham alluded to the British Army's success in the Falkland Islands in 1982 and the U.S. intervention in Grenada in 1983.

He stated that these light infantry divisions (LIDs) would be better suited for low-intensity combat operations and that LIDs would give the United States the ability to meet any crisis, as these units would possess greater tactical mobility in more restrictive environments and in any type of weather. The arguments for and against this concept, while not expressed on the surface of the discussions at Leavenworth, certainly were mumbled and grumbled by some DeVos met at Leavenworth.

* * * * *

Bell Hall was the site of the meeting at Leavenworth and it was chaired by the DA action officers who, with the CSA's guidance, tried to keep the meetings moving forward to develop a division TO&E rather than argue the concept itself. The driving force behind these organizational changes was, as outlined in the *White Paper*, to reduce the size of an infantry division from its current structure of sixteen thousand soldiers down to around ten thousand, thereby increasing the ability for such a division to be deployed in five-hundred C-141 sorties or less. Since the basic fighting unit the entire concept revolved around was the infantry battalion, this meant reorganizing those battalions from seven hundred soldiers and one hundred vehicles down to around five hundred soldiers and thirty vehicles. Needless to say, this reduction in vehicles meant less anti-tank assets, smaller mortars, less medical, signal, and support vehicles and more reliance at the infantry company level for leaders and soldiers who were adaptable to the situations they might face.

To Ed, this meant that the more skilled and independent leaders you could have in these light infantry battalions, the better chance you had to achieve success in the variety of missions that could be thrown their way. To him, the answer was obvious: build these units around Ranger qualified soldiers, or at least better trained soldiers who had many of those same skills seen in Ranger qualified soldiers.

As predicted by General Moore, not all those in attendance at this meeting were ready to jump on board. Those individuals who came from the perspective of having heavy mechanized and/or armor experience were aghast as they could envision over time prestige, power, and promotions shifting to these LIDs. Like any major change in any large organization, there was some "dragging of the feet" just because it was a change, taking some out of their comfort zone. Personnel people were concerned how to provide manpower for the LIDs as the CSA envisioned having five light infantry divisions—two to be reorganized: the 7th and the 25th; creating two new divisions—the 6th and the 10th Mountain; as well as converting the 29th, a National Guard Division, to this new structure.

After a day or two, with the DA action officers addressing and then readdressing the purpose of the meeting, the recommendations for the TO&E of these divisions were hammered out. Some of the struggles of the specifics of the LID's organization were valid because normally the operational concept of how a unit fights and the accompanying doctrine they would employ would be established first and then the development of the TO&E would follow. In this case, to meet the CSA's guidance to get the LID concept moving quickly, the TO&E came first and the specific doctrine and field manuals (FM) would follow. Because this was not the normal way of doing business, some leaned back on that age-old slogan, "We've never done it this way before." Fortunately, the Infantry School representatives and Ed were much alike in their thinking and so the recommended infantry battalion structure and much of the division's combat, combat support, and combat service support units' TO&Es seemed, at least in this first cut, to be suitable. Once copies of the hand-drawn TO&E for the LIDs were provided, DeVos flew back to Fort Ord.

Upon his arrival, Ed called the CG's office and soon found himself in General Moore's office, the debrief taking a good hour because of the CG's questions. Overall, the man seemed satisfied the direction the LID was taking. Ed was almost out the door when General Moore stopped him. "Oh, I almost forgot to tell you. We (the 7th Infantry Division) will be the first division to be restructured. We'll start with one infantry battalion and then we'll restructure a brigade and its combat support elements. The rest of the division will follow based on how it goes with that first battalion and the brigade. Once that first battalion has reduced its size down to this new TO&E, you will be the XO of that battalion. It will be 2-32 Infantry. Congratulations. Keep up the good work."

As DeVos stumbled to his car, all he could think about that late April day in 1984 was the discussion he had with the V Corps G-1 three years earlier. What an opportunity. To be with soldiers at an Infantry Battalion again. God had truly smiled on him this day.

To better understand the issues that 2-32 Infantry would face in terms of physical preparedness, Ed took a page out of Stephen Ambrose's book, *Pegasus Bridge*, the story of the mission to take this critical bridge on D-Day, 6 June 1944. As Ambrose described it, British Major John Howard, the commander of that unit and no relation to the John Howard in the 7th Infantry Division, trained his men to be able to road march twelve miles in two hours, a remarkable feat when soldiers are weighed down by their fifty-sixty pound rucksack. With that in mind, in his last months as the Brigade S-3, DeVos trained his officers and NCOs up to meet that same standard. For those who might like the challenge, you "dog-trot" on all the flats and on all the down hills, and you walk really fast up the hills.

* * * * *

Most of life's lessons don't come from a book. Some may come from a quick impassioned comment from someone you respect when they say, "Just keep doing your best and it will all work out."

Sometimes life's greatest lessons can come to you totally out of nowhere in the form of an unexpected gift. On the day before Ed moved from the Brigade S-3 position to 2-32 Infantry, all the officers and NCOs he had served with at the Brigade S-3 shop surprised him with a gift—a brand new Bible and each of these men had written a comment or two on the inside cover. It was DeVos' routine to arrive around 0600 each morning and spend some quiet time in his office to read his Bible and go through a daily devotional. To his recollection, he never mentioned that to anyone, yet, without his knowledge, others had been watching.

It was also interesting to note that during these days, his officer's efficiency reports started to have comments in them about his Christian values and morals, something not seen too often. Experiences like these cause one to always remember that, as a leader, you are always being watched. As a leader, like it or not, you are a role model. Do your words equal your actions? It is also a reminder that, "The higher up the flag pole you go, the more your backside shows."

As Ed looked back on the last four years as he moved a small box of items to his new office in 2-32 Infantry, he could see God's leading: first, getting to leave Germany a year early. Then there was the assignment to Fort Ord even though he and the family would have preferred going back to Fort Benning. Then there was the wise counseling from Colonel Howard and General Moore—"Hang in there." "Do your best and it will all work out."

So simple, yet sometimes so difficult. "Do your best and it will all work out."

12. FORT ORD, CALIFORNIA.
THE CHIEF OF STAFF'S DREAM

While DeVos went about his business as the 2nd Brigade S-3 for the next two months, he stayed away from 2-32 Infantry as it was not his place to interfere in any way, shape, or form, as the battalion began the process of downsizing and restructuring. Major "Buzz" Sherwood, 2-32's XO, had the bulk of that responsibility which required reducing the number of vehicles in the battalion from one hundred down to around thirty-five in three months, a monumental maintenance effort which Buzz and his team of soldiers did well. Simultaneously, the battalion was reducing the number of soldiers in the unit down to the five-hundred-man level by stabilizing those men they could for up to eighteen months to help build cohesion. Buzz's efforts did not go unrewarded, as several years later he commanded 2-22 Infantry in the 10th Mountain Division.

The history of the 2nd Battalion of 32nd Infantry and the 32nd Regiment closely parallels the history of the 7th Infantry Division in World War I, World War II, and the Korean conflict. Known as the "The Queen's Own," this title was given to the regiment by Queen Liliuoka-lani when the regiment was formed in Oahu, Hawaii in 1916. In 1984, the unit's greeting was "Buccaneers, by God." Through the years since then, two of the 32nd Infantry's three battalions have been deactivated due to the Army's downsizing. Currently, the 1st Battalion of the 32nd Regiment remains on active duty as part of the 10th Mountain Division at Fort Drum, New York.

When Ed joined the battalion in June 1984, LTC Joe Windle was the battalion commander, an enthusiastic leader, full of energy. A proud graduate of Auburn University, the cry "War Eagle" was dominant during football season. At last check, Joe retired as a Colonel after commanding a brigade in the 9th Infantry Division at Fort Lewis, Washington. The unit's Command Sergeant Major was CSM Johnnie Washington, a man who was awarded the Distinguished Service Cross for his service in Vietnam when he was in the 4th Infantry Division. A seasoned veteran, the Command Sergeant Major was always watching out for his solders, pushing them at the right times, correcting them at other times, and always encouraging them to do their best. The four company commanders were excited about the challenge of being in the Army's first light battalion and took great pride in having that opportunity.

As training plans were developed, it became apparent that with fewer vehicles to maintain, this freed up a lot of soldier time to focus on more individual and team skills required in the lighter, more maneuverable battalion. The downsizing served to emphasize that a big change was taking place, not only in the battalion but in the division as well. It was clear that these changes were not just words as soldiers and officers sensed a transformation.

During this train-up phase, the 2-32 Infantry took time to give its squad and team leaders additional training to increase their war fighting skills so that they, in turn, could better train their soldiers. The goal of this was to drive the point home that the battalion was the forerunner for the rest of the Army in light infantry tactics and techniques. All this came with a heavy dose of night training. Eventually, a "Light Fighters" course morphed into a pre-Ranger course for those wishing to volunteer for Ranger School as more and more slots became available to the division through the cooperation of the Infantry School at Fort Benning and TRADOC headquarters. With the passage of time, and more units in the division transitioned to the light TO&E, the number of Ranger School slots increased, benefitting not only Fort Ord units, but later the 10th Mountain and the 25th Infantry Divisions.

Within 2-32 Infantry, rifle marksmanship, day and night land navigation, squad tactics, and physical training received more and more emphasis. With these important training thoughts clear, a wealth of ideas came from inside the battalion. On at least two occasions, the battalion leadership—Joe Windle, the four company commanders, CSM Washington, and DeVos—hosted several visitors in the battalion conference room to discuss the specifics of what the battalion was doing and how "we" were implementing the guidance of the CSA's *White Paper*. These meetings, normally an hour or so in length, were chaired by the CSA, General Wickham, with MG Moore at his side. As the battalion progressed in tune with General Wickham's vision, it was gratifying to watch him dialogue with the company commanders as he encouraged them and taught them about the reasons for paving the way for others to follow. Needless to say, these gatherings were "heady" experiences as everyone at the table had the opportunity to have their voices heard.

As the squads and then platoons began to show proficiency in the skills envisioned, the battalion moved more to night operations at Hunter Liggett. At times, it seemed that the battalion spent more time there than at Fort Ord, with DeVos and Windle investing many nights walking through the woods, assessing how the squads and platoons were developing, making corrections and improvements as required.

As part of the unit's role as the lead battalion in the division, 2-32 Infantry was the first battalion to turn in all its M151 jeeps, which had been in the Army's inventory since 1951, for the brand new HUMVEEs (high mobility multipurpose wheeled vehicle), a much larger four wheel drive vehicle with remarkable stability. Ed personally experienced the difference between the two vehicles because the night before the HUM-VEEs were issued to the battalion, he was on a very steep, winding road at Hunter Liggett, holding on for dear life in an M151. The next day, riding on that same goat path in a HUMVEE, it was like traveling on a smooth interstate highway. With the size and maneuverability of the HUMVEE, these vehicles helped fill the gap of the loss of the previous larger vehicle fleet.

As the battalion's training continued to evolve and sergeants' provided more and more practical input and ideas, the battalion got more creative in developing unit code words, tactics, and ways to reduce its logistical tail which, if not carefully orchestrated, could give away well-hidden unit locations. To reduce vehicle dependency, the battalion reduced rations to two MREs per day instead of three, thereby reducing the soldier load in his rucksack for four and five-day missions. The squads also got very good at caching their heavy rucksacks if the situation allowed. During one Hunter Liggett deployment, each squad was given live chickens and rabbits, some potatoes, and carrots as their rations for the next twen-ty-four hours. The farm boys in the squads quickly became the most valuable soldiers as they showed their fellow city-dweller soldiers how to make short work of a chicken. It should be noted that in a few squads, some of the "bunnies" mysteriously got away before becoming dinner. There was no report of any chickens escaping.

To help keep the battalion's families apprised of what all this training was about and to answer the questions about what their loved ones did in the field, on one Hunter Liggett deployment the battalion held a "family day" where the moms and children were bussed down to the training area. It was a fun day for all with some rappelling demonstrations, a short hands-on land navigation course for the kids, painting camou-flage on the children's faces, a hand-to-hand combat demonstration, and some other activities, all before serving the families a delicious MRE (Meals Ready to Eat) lunch. The younger kids like Ed's son, Keith, now ten-years old, were thrilled and couldn't get enough of the whole experience. Some moms, on the other hand, had their fill of the dust and dirt that swirled around them on that hot, windy day. It probably didn't help that the MREs were cold. Overall, the day was a great success and a morale builder for the soldiers.

* * * *

Before the transition, almost all deployments to Hunter Liggett were in large vehicle convoys, but as training progressed, the battalion began to receive division helicopter assets to deploy into the training area in both day and night insertions. Because of the distance and the number of helicopters to transport the entire battalion, platoon and company air assaults became the norm.

In time, the battalion made several larger unit insertions into the dirt strip at Hunter Liggett on Air Force C-130s. These aircraft were staged on the northern side of the Monterey Regional Airport in a space which could accommodate up to three of these aircraft at any one time. At first, these air insertions were conducted in the daytime, but as the training exercises increased in complexity, night time flights into Hunter Liggett in the C-130s became more exciting.

One night DeVos sat right behind a young pilot and his co-pilot, each of whom looked like they were twenty-years old. During the flight, each of these pilots wore NVGs (night vision goggles) as they landed their four-engine propeller driven transport onto Liggett's dirt strip in total blackout conditions. After a great sigh of relief, particularly from the soldiers in the back of the airplane, as soon as the crew chief lowered the ramp, the soldiers did not look back as they scampered out into the darkness.

* * * *

To give the men of 2-32 Infantry a different view of the world and to get away from the dust, dirt, and some of the torrential rains that occasionally pounded Hunter Liggett as they came off the Pacific Ocean fifteen miles to the west, the battalion traveled by bus to Coronado, California, south of San Diego, almost at the U.S. and Mexican border, for four days of training at the Navy's Amphibious Base.

From DeVos' perspective, this was a most unusual opportunity because from the LID discussions that he participated in at Fort Leavenworth, it was clear that the Marines were concerned that these new, lighter, more mobile Army units might, at some point, be called upon to conduct amphibious assaults, missions the Marines strongly defended because they felt that was their "turf," and theirs alone. The Marines view of amphibious assaults as exclusive to them is interesting because history is filled with numerous accounts of amphibious assaults made by Army units in World War II at places such as North Africa, Sicily, Italy, Southern France and, of course, D-Day. In addition to those assaults, the 7th Infantry Division was part of the Inchon amphibious landing during the Korean War.

Despite the "political" concerns at some higher level, the Navy treated the battalion very well. The quarters for the soldiers and the NCOs were more than adequate and the officers stayed in one of the two six-story high-rise BOQs. Because the training ended late in the afternoons, there was sufficient time for soldiers to explore the local surroundings near the base, something far different from many Army posts. DeVos and Joe Windle even had time one evening to go out and eat at one of the high-end restaurants nearby, a totally different experience from the crusty ground at Hunter Liggett.

The amphibious training the unit received was a combination of physical training, use of rubberized assault boats called RB-15s, like those Ed had been introduced to in Ranger School, staff instruction on cross-loading men and equipment on various landing crafts, all leading to boarding one of the Navy's large amphibious assault ships to conduct an actual beach assault on the last day of training. For the officers and men of 2-32 Infantry, it was a thrill to be aboard a ship so large that all the assault landing craft were housed inside the ship itself, allowing the soldiers to board their landing crafts without having to climb down cargo nets in the pitching seas of the open ocean as was done in World War II and Korea.

For the officers, the biggest shock came when they were invited to eat in the "Officers' Mess," where menus were handed to each officer by the immaculately dressed stewards as they sat down at tables adorned with white table clothes and silverware. It was also hard not to stare at the paintings on the walls of the mess which paid homage to some of the Navy's great victories and many of Navy's great war-time leaders.

After lunch, the beach landing took place. While some additional training would be required if the battalion was to conduct another amphibious assault, the experience of working with the Navy for those few days was the source of great conversation for many days.

A few months later, the battalion returned to southern California, this time spending two days at Camp Pendleton, the large Marine Corps base north of San Diego, where the soldiers of the battalion concentrated on MOUT (Military Operations in Urbanized Terrain) training, a very difficult tactical environment where every door and every window can conceal an enemy. This was followed by an exhilarating and invigorating day learning quick-kill techniques on a range designed specifically for this type of engagement.

* * * * *

While 2-32 Infantry concentrated on its mission, the restructuring of the rest of the division's units began to accelerate as more thought and energy was directed toward deploying the division on short notice. Since the requirement of the division was to have the first infantry battalion "wheels up" in eighteen hours from the initial alert notification and then follow that unit with the remainder of the division, the coordination and plans to meet that goal became top priority at division headquarters. Because the designated U.S. Air Force airfield the division would deploy from was four hours driving distance away from Fort Ord, this meant the first deploying infantry battalion would have its vehicles packed with equipment, ammunition, water, fuel, rations, and all other necessary equipment at all times.

While the deployment requirements to meet any contingency became the division's first priority, the world did not stop. Training still needed to be conducted, taskings to support post and community still needed to be met, and soldiers still needed time to attend Army schools, take leave, and get some time off. Thus, a system needed to be developed for the long run to sustain the ability to meet the LID contingency at any time and to train to accomplish that mission. Using the model of the 82nd Airborne Division, the first battalion to be deployed was called DRF1, for Division Ready Force 1. The second battalion that would follow the first was DRF2; the third DRF3.

Within the 7th Infantry Division with its two brigades of three battalions each, the brigade which commanded the DRF1, DRF2 and DRF3 battalions, was designated as DRB1 for Division Ready Brigade 1, meaning if required, this would be the first brigade headquarters to deploy. The other brigade and its subordinate battalions were designated as DRB2, and could be deployed, if necessary, after DRB1. DRBs would rotate every ninety days. The DRFs within the DRBs would rotate every thirty days.

This rotation of units meant that the DRF1 stayed on Fort Ord proper and would do all of their training on post since an alert could be called at any time, day or night, on weekdays, weekends, or holidays. A telephone alert system was established in each unit so the units could be assembled and begin drawing weapons and other sensitive items within two hours of notification. For the DRF1, there would be additional personnel checks, operations orders to be given, all before the vehicle convoy headed for the departure airfield. This convoy, along with buses and truck loads of soldiers, would leave for the departure airfield within eight hours to insure that the loading process of the C-141s at the departure airfield could be accomplished in time to meet the requirement of being "wheels up" within eighteen hours of the initial alert notification.

Because the DRF2 and DRF3 units had more time to react to an alert, they were able to conduct training at Hunter Liggett. Likewise, DRB2 battalions could conduct off post training as well, although their units would also be the ones to receive all the taskings from G3 Ops which had been discussed earlier. This system insured that DRB1 units could focus on deployment and training while DRB2 units concerned themselves with support taskings as well as training. This would also be the best time for DRB2 soldiers to take leave, attend schools, etc. All combat support and combat service support elements in the division which supported the two brigades followed their supported brigade's schedule.

As the battalions rotated through this schedule, they always knew that during their DRF1 cycle, they would get some kind of an alert to help test their systems and timing to make sure they could meet the eighteen-hour window. While this was new to some commanders, those who had experience in the 82nd Airborne Division or who had been stationed in Europe were quite familiar with a similar alert system and the reasons for it. Once this system was established and understood by all, the prudent commanders exercised some type of a unit alert before they deployed to Hunter Liggett or other training site.

* * * * *

Late in 1984, DeVos flew to South Korea to coordinate the battalion's role in Team Spirit '85, which would be a walk-through of the LID's first battalion's ability to meet the CSA's guidance of rapid deployment to a critical area. While much of what was to occur was well-known by all participants, it was the concept that everyone wanted to see. For 2-32 Infantry, this meant the battalion would be on DRF1 in the run-up to Team Spirit '85. The unit would then receive an alert notification, move all its personnel and equipment to the departure airfield where the first airplane would launch under the eighteen hour goal. The reminder of the battalion would be right behind that first aircraft, each one flying non-stop to South Korea as they would be refueled in the air, making this about an eighteen hour flight. After landing at a U.S. Air Force airbase in South Korea, the soldiers and their equipment would immediately be loaded onto C-130s and flown directly into the exercise area, landing on a dirt strip, either day or night. Once the alert was called, the battalion would be digging foxholes in South Korea within forty hours, depending on efficiency of the Air Force's aircraft.

A great deal was riding on this deployment as it was General Wickham's vision of the Light Infantry Division concept put into action. There would be many more "tests" that would follow this first one in the months that followed. Each one was proving the restructuring, the training, and the purpose of the LIDs made the U.S. Army a stronger and more flexible force.

* * * * *

For 2-32 Infantry, Team Spirit '85 demonstrated that there was a role for light infantry, not only in terms of rapid deployment but in the tough, rugged, and cold terrain of the Korean peninsula.

For DeVos, this exercise had two highlights worthy of note. First, at almost the last minute, the Air Force changed its transport planes that would fly the battalion to Korea from C-141 Starlifters to C-5 Galaxies, an aircraft with almost five times the lift capacity of a C-141. While this change would mean fewer airplanes would be needed, this late notification caused the battalion staff to quickly reconfigure the aircraft loads, which they did in a most efficient manner. Not an easy thing to do in the days before computers.

Second, Ed ran into a man he still calls the smartest general officer he ever met. Near the final day of Team Spirit '85, 2-32 Infantry was ordered to make a night river crossing of a major river in boats provided by the South Korean Army (ROKs). This crossing was to take place at 0200 to surprise the opposing force on the other side of the river. Ed, as the one in charge of this crossing site, arrived at the correct location several hours early to make sure the ROKs were prepared to accomplish their mission. Upon his arrival, it was clear the ROK engineer unit was not having a good night, making the probability of crossing the river on time seem highly unlikely. As he ranted and raved through an interpreter at the ROKs, their progress picked up speed, but the U.S. major was still irate.

Driving up in the middle of this scene appeared a U.S. brigadier general, who jumped out of his jeep and came over to the major. "How's it going? Everything track?"

At this point, barely recognizing the man's rank, DeVos held nothing back, telling him the "blank, blank" ROKs were screwed up and he was "lighting a fire under 'em." The general took in the scene for a minute or so before he nodded and said, "Looks like to me, Major, you've got the situation well under control. So, I'll be on my way. Good night." Hopping back in his jeep, the man left without another word.

Ed never found out the man's name, but in the years that followed, he has always felt that this general realized he couldn't do any more than what the other officer was already doing, so there was no reason for him to hang around and get in the way. A wise general officer.

* * * * *

Once the battalion returned to Fort Ord in late March 1985, the pace of activity did not slow down. First, Ed soon found himself on a plane to Fort McCoy, Wisconsin again to evaluate a National Guard infantry unit. Second, a number of significant changes of command took place at Fort Ord as MG Moore's time as the division commander came to an end and he was replaced by another great infantryman, MG William Harrison. Also, Colonel Harris, the 2nd Brigade Commander, was replaced by Colonel John Howard. Then, to top everything off, Ed's name appeared on the promotion list for Lieutenant Colonel, which meant he would have to leave the XO position in 2-32 Infantry and be reassigned into an LTC slot which turned out to be the XO of the 2nd Brigade of the Army's first light infantry brigade.

The marching orders in this position became clear as soon as Ed's transfer back to the brigade headquarters was complete. While the battalion had successfully deployed and fought in the difficult, mountainous terrain of Korea, could that same unit, or another one like it, successfully fight alongside a heavy mechanized or armor unit in a much larger, faster moving battlefield against a battle-tested, savvy opponent? It was a fair question, one which the heavy mechanized and the armor communities had raised when the *White Paper* was published.

The best place to test this mix of tactics and capabilities was at a location familiar to most state-side heavy mechanized and armor forces: The National Training Center (NTC) at Fort Irwin, California. This post, which occupies one thousand square miles in the Mojave Desert south of Death Valley, is located thirty-five miles north of Barstow, California. In 1979, DA directed that this ground become the NTC because, with its vast expanse of land, mechanized infantry and armor units could conduct maneuvers there against an organized opposing force (OPFOR) who had the advantage of knowing the terrain.

While this high desert environment was one light infantry typically avoided, in fairness, the ability of LIDs to fight in such an austere setting needed to be addressed. Because the other two battalions of the 2nd Brigade had restructured from the older TO&E to the LID TO&E, 1-32 Infantry was designated as the unit that would deploy to the NTC and fight together with an armored unit against the OPFOR in April/May1986. Once Colonel Howard made that decision, DeVos turned the brigade staff toward supporting that unit with all they had.

With 1-32 Infantry focused on Fort Irwin, like 2-32 Infantry earlier, this unit spent a great deal of time at Hunter Liggett. To prepare for this deployment, DeVos and members of both the battalion and brigade staffs made several reconnaissance trips to Fort Irwin, a four-hundred-mile journey to the southeast, once by helicopter and once by vehicle to get familiarized with the ten- hour convoy route. These recons proved to be most helpful because even a good map reader cannot appreciate all the folds in the ground that light infantrymen can use to their advantage, not only in the night, but in the daytime as well. While there were some wide-open spaces where you could see for many miles, even within those flat areas, there were some opportunities 'Light Fighters' could exploit to their advantage.

As all good infantrymen know, "One look is worth ten thousand words." As DeVos learned from Team Spirit '84, to do a proper light infantry reconnaissance, it must be done on the ground, not just from an aerial view or a map.

* * * * *

When the days came for the Heavy-Light rotation at NTC, as antici-pated, 1-32 Infantry acquitted itself very well. While there were some areas where improvements needed to be made, overall, the battalion, the brigade, and the supporting division elements that made up the task force performed well. Even though the "heavy community" was looking for the light infantry to stumble in their "backyard," they were surprised by the agility and ability of the light infantrymen to move about the battlefield, showing up at unexpected places and times, doing significant damage to the surprised OPFOR.

One bit of drama occurred near the end of the exercise when the OH-58 (a light observation helicopter) that Colonel Howard was riding in lost power and crashed. Once the helicopter was located, it was determined that, along with the pilot, he would require some medical attention not available at Fort Irwin. MG Harrison, who was at Fort Irwin as an "interested observer," told Major (P) DeVos that he was now the acting Brigade Commander and he was to "continue the march," which meant finish the exercise, and then redeploy the task force back to Fort Ord as planned. Those orders were followed, and everyone made it back to home station on schedule. As expected, Colonel Howard returned to duty five days later, although he was a little gimpy for another week or so.

A few weeks later, Ed was finishing a proposed article he was submitting to the *Infantry Magazine* for publication when he was told that there was a phone call for him in Colonel Howard's office—a strange occurrence. Even though he knew that he had been selected to command an infantry battalion, this phone call was a Godsend as it set in motion the next three years of his military career. The caller was MG Bill Carpenter, CG of the 10th Mountain Division. His was calling to congratulate Ed on making this list and to inform him that he would be the battalion commander of 1-87 Infantry, a battalion that would be activated in May 1987.

The plan was for Ed and Susan to relocate their family to Fort Drum, just east of Watertown, New York, not later than 1 September 1986. Once there, he would build the battalion from the ground up, meaning he would be the first man in the unit, his CSM would be the second. They would then train the officers and NCOs the personnel system would send them, and activate the battalion in early May 1987 when the young soldiers who had just completed basic and advanced infantry training together at Fort Benning in a program called COHORT would arrive at Fort Drum. Then his official command tour of two years would begin.

* * * * *

Things began to move quickly. First, there was a quick four-day trip for Ed and Susan to fly to New York to see about quarters. Since Fort Drum at this time had little in the way of military housing, the DeVos' contracted to have a house built outside of Watertown, a ten-minute drive from where the battalion headquarters would be located. During this trip, they were introduced to some of the others at the post. What allowed all this to take place was the flexibility of Ed's parents to ride herd on Kristen and Keith as Ed and Susan made this trip to New York. They also stayed a bit longer to witness Ed's promotion to LTC and enjoy his promotion party, an event that was blessed as one of Ed's soldiers generously provided a large freshly caught Alaskan salmon which the mess sergeants prepared to perfection.

Preparations for the move then began in earnest: packing, getting all the school papers to get Kristen (a rising high school freshman) and Keith enrolled properly into the Watertown School District, and figuring out the timing to drive from California to New York, a distance of three thousand miles. Complicating all this was that Colonel Howard would be changing command early. His next assignment to be the Secretary of the Army Chief of Staff's office in the Pentagon had been speeded up to mid-July 1986, instead of early August. It was not possible for Howard's replacement, Colonel Rich Timmons, a man Ed knew from 3-7 Infantry days at Fort Benning, to arrive in time for the mid-July date. Another wrinkle was that brigade would be in the field for a ten-day planned exercise at Hunter Liggett near the time that Colonel Howard needed to be packing. In light of these circumstances, Colonel Howard presented a plan to coordinate the Howard/Timmons change of command along with the brigade exercise at Hunter Liggett to MG Harrison. After a few questions, the CG agreed with the colonel's proposal.

That recommendation consisted of two parts. First, the 2nd Brigade would go to the field as scheduled, putting all three of its battalions through the paces that Colonel Howard had previously approved. Second, there would be a brigade change of command in the field with the CG accepting the brigade colors from Colonel Howard and then passing them to LTC DeVos. Two weeks later, there would be another change of command, this one a more formal affair, where the brigade's colors would pass from DeVos to Colonel Timmons. Three days later the DeVos' were on their way to Fort Drum, taking with them many memories of the units, the friends, the numerous deployments, and the understanding of the Light Infantry Division few others had. In the years that followed, they remembered those days at Fort Ord as some of the best days of their lives. But there was one thing they would not miss — earthquakes — the ones that rolled, the ones that seemed to bounce the ground under your feet, the ones that shook the house, rattling the windows.

* * * * *

In four years the learning never stopped, because with building something new, there were always lessons to be learned. But for the last two years at Fort Ord, three major thoughts dominated DeVos' thinking as he packed his last items out of his office.

First, the core of the Light Infantry is the squad. Good, well trained squads can make up for the mistakes — both major and minor — of those above them. If the squad leader is given mission-type orders, he will find a way to get the job done. Leaders higher up the chain of command must understand that, at some point, the squads may use their initiative in creative ways to accomplish their mission which will require the chain of command to back them up and not be too critical of their more unconventional approaches to succeed. If you want your NCOs to exercise some freedom to get the job done, be prepared for the creativity they may exhibit.

Second, leaders at all levels might consider that encounter DeVos had with that unknown general officer in Korea. If you come upon leaders below your pay grade who are doing everything you would do, pat them on the back. Tell them they are doing a good job and then get out of their way. Go find someone else who needs your help, your counsel, or your wisdom. Don't waste your valuable time helping those leaders who don't need to be helped.

Third, there are not enough words that can adequately express the role military spouses play in the success of our Armed Forces. Because of the nature of the military, the service members can be gone at the "drop of a hat," to far-off locations that are hard to spell and are not easily found on a map, without any specifics of when they will return. When these deployments occur, whatever the family is involved in—school, athletic events, sickness, family concerns, financial issues, car problems, leaking toilets, carrying groceries up four flights of stairs, etc.—have now been dropped into the spouse's lap with little or no prior warning.

The lesson here is that the wise service member, enlisted or officer, should never take his or her spouse for granted. No matter how well they keep up a good front, the emotions and ups and downs the spouses experience when the service member is away runs the gamut: from being fearful to looking forward to a joyful return; from moments of despair and doubt wondering if all this time alone was what they signed up for, to remembering their deep love for each other and their vows to be help mates; from feeling discouraged yet having to be an encourager to others; from feeling lonely to being the rock to the children for an undetermined length of time; from being the decision maker one day and being the disciplinarian the next; from being the daily letter writer to praying for the safe return of their one true love; from being a counselor one day and the authoritarian the next; from being the dressed up spouse at the grand unit gathering one evening to scrubbing the floors the next morning; from being the charming hostess one night to washing the dog the next afternoon; from chauffeuring a child to their soccer practice on Saturday morning and then leading a women's Bible Study that evening; from removing two feet of snow out of the driveway with a snow blower to warding off the fears and wiping away the tears in order to comfort a child missing dad or mom that night; from writing the monthly bills to always being the on-call nurse. The list goes on and on.

As the deployments piled up and the time away from the family increased, Ed's appreciation grew deeper and deeper for how his family—Susan, Kristen, and Keith—served their country in ways few others could ever understand. His ability to serve his country was made possible through the team effort of his family. For that he will always be grateful.

13. FORT DRUM, NEW YORK.
TRAIN UP AND ACTIVATION

Within a week of the "formal" 2nd Brigade change of command, the DeVos' had their household goods packed and then picked up. They also sold their 1970 VW with 120,000 miles on it to a deserving soldier, and then stuffed their Volvo station wagon to the hilt. The last two things to go in the car that August 1986 morning were the dog and cat. The three thousand mile trek would take around eight days as they planned to drive through Nevada, Utah, Wyoming, Nebraska, Iowa, Illinois, Michigan, and then into Canada, before crossing the St. Lawrence River over the Thousand Islands Bridge to enter the United States and the state of New York, thirty miles north of Watertown.

The drive gave the family a chance to appreciate the vastness and diverse geography of our country. It also confirmed for Ed and Susan that they were not big city folks as the drive around the southside of Chicago proved to be a harrowing experience. By following this route, it gave the family a chance to visit an aunt and uncle who Ed had not seen in years when they spent a night in Grand Rapids, Michigan, the city where he was born.

Those many hours on the road gave this thirty-nine-year-old officer some time to think about several subjects. First, there was his selection to command 1-87 Infantry. While some of the selection process is steeped in mystery, it is generally known that a board of senior officers is convened once a year to select from a large list of eligible lieutenant colonels in all branches to fill the battalion command positions for the next year. Those selected are on a path which normally leads to further advancement, assuming that the individual is successful when he commands his battalion.

It is recognized that all those who are selected for these command positions have (1) outstanding OERs in all their previous assignments, (2) served at some major command, and (3) been with soldiers at either the battalion or brigade level as either an S-3 and/or XO. If an officer has served in one of those positions, it is possible he may be selected. If he has served in two of those positions, he is competitive; in three, he is highly competitive; and if he has served in all four of the positions, the probability he will be selected is extremely high. In DeVos' case, if you count his battalion S-3 time when he was a 1LT in 2-509 Airborne Infantry, he had served in all four of these positions for a total of over four years. Ed knew from all he had dealt with over those years, there weren't many situations or crises he hadn't previously encountered. He was about as prepared for this next assignment as anyone could be. As someone joked with him years later, if he had not been selected to command a battalion, there would have been an investigation.

Thankful for the experiences he had at Fort Ord and at other locations before then, he asked himself what kind of leader he had become? As Ed batted that question back and forth, he came to the conclusion that, if he were asked, he judged himself to be an optimistic realist. He was a "glass half full guy" who was motivated to achieve high goals. He was always looking forward, not backward. While he did not consider himself to be a man of great intellect, he knew he could out-work just about anybody. He had made mistakes along the way, but he had learned something from each one of them. From the Assessment Center tests done years ago at Fort Benning, he knew God had blessed him with a certain presence that caused others to view him as a leader and he understood the phrase, *when in charge, take charge*. Yet, he was wise enough to not put blinders on and charge without first gathering the critical facts. He was open to the thoughts, ideas, and opinions of those around him, knowing that by doing so a team effort was established, quite opposite of those who adhered to the "my way or the highway" approach. This openness also provided a continuous flow of ideas and thoughts from others so improvements and/or adjustments could be made as necessary.

As he continued this journey in self-analysis, Ed thanked God over and over for putting great leaders and mentors in his path. Men like Ted Jenes, Bill Edge, Ross Franklin, Willard Latham, Ken Lucas, Jim Moore, and others who helped mold and shape his thinking. Without their counsel, their guidance, and their example, DeVos would not have this opportunity to be with soldiers once more.

His next thoughts centered on forming a unit from the ground up. As he considered that more and more, he realized this "building a unit from the ground up" did not just apply to him, but to all the other commanders in the 10th Mountain Division, from General Carpenter on down. Imagine, an entire division being birthed this way. Not since World War II. Unprecedented.

Having asked the question at various locations about why this or that was done a certain way, the most irritating answer he received many times was, "We've always done it that way." Now he was about to put things in motion in 1-87 Infantry that those who followed him would say, "We've always done it that way." With that in mind, he felt a keen responsibility to get things right the first time, so he vowed right then to approach even the seemingly small decisions to make sure they would be right for the battalion's long-term benefit. His overriding thoughts were: Don't be hasty. Think first. Avoid knee-jerk reactions.

* * * * *

It was the middle of the afternoon on a beautiful August day when they came to the last checkpoint in Canada before they could re-enter the United States. After a few questions, the border policeman suddenly had some concerns as he noted the California tag on the car, both Ed and Susan's Florida driver's licenses, yet they said they were going to reside in New York but had no address, and they were joy riding through Canada to get there. He did not seem to have any understanding or interest in U.S. military orders. Then when he saw the dog and cat in the back of the car, he wanted to see the health papers on these two ferocious beasts. At that point, Susan, being as polite as she could be, said, "We can do that, but that will require us to unpack the entire back of this car since the papers you want to see are at the bottom of all this." With that, the man shook his head and gave us permission to leave his country.

About an hour later, it got worse when we drove by the lot we had purchased three months earlier, expecting to see our new house just about ready for occupancy. All that was there was a big hole in the ground. The builder had been slowed down by the weather and his own personal management style which meant the DeVos' would not be in our new home until November, just in time for winter to really set in.

This caused this military couple to quickly reorder their thinking. With few alternatives available, the DeVos' moved into the only tempo-rary quarters on Fort Drum—a HUD trailer -until their house would be ready for them to move into. Their neighbors in their nearby HUD trailer were Harley and Sheila Moberg also from Fort Ord. Harley, also a LTC, would be the commander of the 10th Signal Battalion of the 10th Mountain Division.

While this entire story could take up a chapter by itself, suffice to say that for three months, the DeVos' dealt with a runaway mouse who vis-ited them twice early in the morning and "illegally" housing their pets in their trailer. Each day Susan drove the kids to the corner where their new house would be so they could catch the school bus. Then the family made a quick move into their new home before it was completed to make sure that all of their household goods had made it from California. It was a trying several months for the family, but like most military families at one time or the other, they dealt with it and it all turned out in the long run. One of the high points of this period was to see *Top Gun* with the Moberg's at the post theater one afternoon where the National Anthem was played before the movie started.

* * * * *

The area known as Fort Drum today was first called Pine Camp in 1908, a sleepy military training site. It became the training home for three divisions who later deployed to Europe in World War II after a major construction project of over eight hundred buildings was completed during the winter of 1941-1942, one of the coldest on record. In 1951, this installation was renamed Camp Drum for LTG Hugh Drum who served in World War I. It was renamed Fort Drum in 1974 when it became the major training ground for National Guard and Reserve units in the Northeast. The announcement that Fort Drum would be the headquarters of the 10th Mountain Division came in September 1984.

The major town nearest Fort Drum is Watertown, ten miles west of the post, a town of twenty-five thousand in 1986. It was incorporated in 1816, becoming the hub of small industries in this largely rural area with a number of smaller towns around it such as Philadelphia, Lowville, Carthage, Gouverneur, Sackett's Harbor, Adams, and Copenhagen. A decision in 1984 to build housing for military families in some of these smaller towns brought economic growth to the area that is still felt today.

* * * * *

With Susan taking charge of their ever-evolving housing situation, Ed signed in and went to work. The senior leadership in the division in his opinion was unsurpassed. MG Bill Carpenter, known as the "Lonesome End" when he played football at West Point, was a man who spoke little, but when he did, it was always something of value. His chief of staff was Colonel Hugh Shelton, who from 1997 to 2001,was the Chairman of the Joint Chiefs of Staff, the highest- ranking officer in the United States Armed Forces.

Colonel Jack Keane was Ed's boss. He commanded 1st Brigade which consisted of 1-22 and 2-22 Infantry. Zannie Smith, previously stationed with Ed at Fort Ord, commanded "Triple Deuce." Both of these battalions had been activated a year earlier. Jack Keane, a man who Ed holds in high esteem, would later wear four stars in his position as Vice Chief of Staff of the Army. During these early days, Ed met his CSM, Command Sergeant Major Eddie C. DeYampert, a man he grew to trust completely. He was a soldier's soldier.

With the battalion's location and buildings already designated and the basic furniture such as desks, bunks, and chairs in place in their allotted wooden World War II buildings, the ones built forty-five years earlier, these two men were given a once in a lifetime opportunity. Ed was given twelve files of inbound captains from which he could designate as his four company commanders and his staff officers. Likewise, the CSM was given nine files to pick his four first sergeants. After studying the information and talking things through, they made their decisions and never had cause to regret them. During these early days, Ed was TDY for two weeks, attending the Pre-Command Course for battalion and brigade commanders, one week at Fort Leavenworth and another at Fort Benning.

DeVos made two important decisions in these early days. First, the unit slogan would be "To the Top," signifying both the unit's mountain infantry heritage and that the goal of 1-87 Infantry was to be the best battalion in the 10th Mountain Division. Second, although the other two battalions in the brigade had gray PT sweats, 1-87's PT sweats were black with the unit crest on the front and soldier's name and rank on the back. The crest is quite colorful with red, white, and blue framing a mountain in the center. The words at the bottom of the crest—Virus Montesque Vincimus—in Latin mean "We Conquer Powers and Mountains." With their distinctive black PT suits, it was hard to miss the men of this battalion.

By mid-September 1986, the officers and NCOs who were assigned to 1-87 Infantry began to drift in. It was a slow process but by December, most of the battalion's officers and NCOs were on board. With new people coming into the unit every week, DeVos and the CSM held a briefing every Friday afternoon to welcome these new arrivals. Their talks were always the same.

Because these officers and NCOs came from all over the Army, it was incumbent for DeVos to give these new leaders the "Why" of the Light Divisions and to answer every question they had. The second point of emphasis was for DeVos to state, "This is not my battalion. It is not the Sergeant Major's battalion ... It is our battalion. Anything and everything that any one of us does or doesn't do, reflects on all us." Third, the battalion commander told these new members of 1-87 Infantry that if they had experience in what the battalion was about to try, he expected them to step up and tell the chain of command what worked and what didn't so "we" would not repeat the errors others had made. This was all to drive the point home that this battalion "is" a team of professionals climbing to reach its full potential and if "we" worked together, prepared ourselves correctly, worked hard, and learned from our mistakes, "we" *will succeed.*

The fourth and final point of this weekly briefing was to demystify COHORT for everyone and explain its benefits. The genesis of COHORT (cohesion, operational readiness, and training) goes back in our

Army to the World War I and II days when soldiers went through basic training together, deployed to war together as a unit, and were part of their unit for three, four, and sometime five years. While casualties in war took their toll and individual replacements took their place, the core of the unit, the ethos, the culture, and the over-riding philosophy and beliefs remained embedded in those who were there at the beginning. During Vietnam, when our Army sent individual replacements on one-year stints to units across the war zone, this constant flow of new men in some units had a detrimental impact on morale, discipline, and combat effectiveness.

1-87 Infantry, along with its sister infantry battalions in the 10th Mountain Division, would have the advantage of being a COHORT battalion as the historical advantages of this system were clear. Soldiers who went through basic and advanced individual training together could be progressively challenged to be trained in more advanced skills. Long term retention rates would be higher, while discipline issues tended to be much lower. Most importantly, unit pride and cohesiveness would increase because these men knew they would be together for an extended period of time.

As the bulk of the battalion's infantry soldiers went through basic and advanced individual training at Fort Benning, the battalion launched its training program to "train the trainers," a task that began in earnest from January to April 1987. All aspects of infantry training were practiced, drilled, and then drilled again as the officers and NCOs prepared to accept the soldiers from Fort Benning in mid-April. The bulk of this "train the trainer" program was held at Fort Drum, although there was a week when much of the battalion's leadership went to Fort Benning to get a feel for what their in-bound soldiers looked like.

* * * * *

In coordination with all the "higher ups" at brigade and division, the pieces and parts to activate the battalion on 5 May 1987 were set in stone, a date easy for DeVos to remember as he was commissioned on 5 May 1969. Because 1-87 Infantry was the first battalion in the "new" 10th Mountain Division whose flag was flown in the World War II 10th Mountain Division, a great deal of effort was expended to invite the World War II members of the 87th Infantry Regiment to the ceremony. This endeavor paid big dividends. On that day more than eighty men who had served in this regiment in World War II came to the activation ceremony, to include Colonel Ross Wilson, the man who commanded 1-87 Infantry throughout that war. To honor his presence, DeVos made it a point to have Ross take part in the formal part of the activation ceremony as this old soldier once again held the unit colors. Because the 10th Mountain did not have its own division band at that time, a reserve unit was tasked to perform at this ceremony. This was the same band that played for President Ronald Reagan at the Reykjavik Summit in October 1986 in Iceland when he met with Mikhail Gorbachev of the Soviet Union.

To help celebrate that day, the battalion set up a full weapons and equipment display so that the older soldiers could inspect the newer weapons and tell stories to the younger men who were now talking their place. The younger soldiers, particularly those who had just arrived from Fort Benning several weeks earlier, were in awe of these soldiers who were forty, fifty years older. It was a day of excitement and anticipation, coupled with the understanding that this was the beginning of a new chapter in the history of the 1st Battalion, 87th Infantry (Light).

For DeVos, it was the official beginning of the privilege he had to be with these soldiers — infantry soldiers — for another seven hundred and thirty days. This was his goal when he came into the Army. To command an infantry battalion. To him, there was no higher calling. All the days before had prepared him for this. Others had taught him and encouraged him so he could have this opportunity. He was blessed, thankful, and humbled. He knew he was at this place to serve, not to be served. What an honor. What a privilege.

* * * * **

In looking back, there were some things DeVos wished he had done in the train-up time of the unit, and therefore, these thoughts fall into the lessons learned category.

First, while Ed undoubtedly had a wealth of knowledge and understanding about the Light Infantry concept and all the reasons for the unit, he could have been more organized and given more thought to train his officers and NCOs on more details about how to take advantage of their unique skill set to "fight" the unit more effectively. He could have had more "classroom" instruction using sand tables and walk-throughs to help others learn what he had learned. While this knowledge was passed on to his subordinate leaders as time went on, if he had held more formal organized discussions during the train-up, it would have saved him time and effort when the battalion was in the execution part of its existence.

Second, and this would have been so simple, he should have given a copy of the Chief of Staff's *White Paper* to every leader instead of just talking about it. That way it would have been easier to dialogue with his leaders since everyone would be coming at the subject knowing the CSA's viewpoint instead of what they heard DeVos and others say about it.

While the overall activation and train-up period of 1-87 Infantry received high marks from those outside the battalion, Ed knew it could have been even better. The lesson here is don't judge yourself by other's standards. Judge yourself by your standards. If you are honest with yourself, you will know when you have done things to the best of your ability, and when you have not. If you do your best, you can live your life without having as many regrets.

14. FORT DRUM, NEW YORK. CLIMBING TO THE TOP

Photos taken at the activation ceremony of 1-87 Infantry on 5 May 1987 on the 10th Mountain Division parade field would look very much like the ones taken of this same battalion on 5 May 1989 when the command of the battalion changed hands from one officer to another. But if you had a discerning, practiced eye, you would see some subtle differences between the two pictures.

The soldiers in the second photo, the one taken in 1989, stood a little taller. They were physically more imposing. There was steel and seriousness in their eyes that replaced excitement two years before. These men in the 1989 photo were stronger in spirit and mentally tougher; confident both in themselves and in their fellow soldiers who stood to their left and to their right. Each man in that second photo wanted to be the best he could because he did not want to let his friends down; these men counted on each other. Each soldier had made his share of mistakes in the last two years, but they had learned from them, grown because of them, and had matured because of them.

In the 1987 picture, there were twenty-five Army Rangers in 1-87 Infantry. In the 1989 picture, if you counted them, you would see more than fifty men standing in the formation facing the reviewing stand who wore U.S. Army Rangers Tabs. You would also see twenty more soldiers in the 1989 photo wearing the coveted Expert Infantrymen's Badge on their chests than those in the 1987 photo. By all accounts, the battalion that was photographed in May 1989 was one of the best Infantry battalions in the United States Army.

How did these men achieve such results? To understand this transformation, it is necessary to look at those two years in 1-87 Infantry in three ways: its organizational principles, its training philosophy, and the exercises and deployments the battalion took part in.

* * * * *

Organization. From the outside, 1-87 Infantry looked just like the other two infantry battalions of the 1st Brigade, 10th Mountain Division. Each had the same number of personnel, the same number of vehicles. All were housed in the World War II buildings. The rules and regulations for each unit were the same, but something was different. What exactly those differences were no one can really say but…

From the earliest days in the train-up phase until he left command of 1-87 Infantry in May 1989, DeVos told his subordinate leaders that, "When you're in garrison, you're in garrison. When you're in the field, you're in the field," meaning that when the unit was in garrison, PT formations would not begin before 0700. The mess hall would serve breakfast from 0830 to 0930. Training would take place in the company areas after that. Battalion PT uniforms could be worn all day as long as the unit was in garrison. Training was to be finished not later than 1600. On the other hand, "When you're in the field, you're in the field" meant that when the unit crossed the road into the training areas, it was a 24/7 work ethic.

If the battalion was not deployed or in the field, each Monday morning at 1000 the battalion leadership, staff, and the company commanders met to discuss any and all matters of importance to the battalion. This meeting would last no longer than one hour. Each Friday afternoon at 1300, the "Big Four" had a meeting—the battalion commander, the XO, the S-3, and the CSM. For no more than an hour, these four men discussed what had gone right in the last week, what had gone wrong, what fixes needed to be made, and what things needed to be checked before the end of day for next week's training to be a success. The battalion commander assigned each of the four of them specific duties with regard to matters that needed to be checked in the next hour so they wouldn't step on each other's toes.

Every payday, 1-87 Infantry reserved the post theater at 1000 for one hour. This was a combination of awards and decorations, a briefing by the battalion commander about what was coming up in the next two or three months, and a chance for the soldiers to be reminded they were part of a team, a battalion that cared for them. It was a time for team and individuals to be recognized for their accomplishments. Unless something unusual was happening, soldiers were cut loose for the day once they marched back to the battalion area.

Military schooling was emphasized in the battalion from Day One. CSM DeYampert was "like stink on a dog" with his NCOs, making sure they attended every leadership school they could. He accepted no excuses from any soldier who wished to delay attendance to any professional development school because, as the CSM stated, both the soldier and the battalion would benefit from this increase in knowledge. In the May 1989 Change of Command program in the Current History of 1-87 Infantry of the battalion, it states, "Since activation, the battalion has graduated over 400 soldiers from schools ranging from PLDC (Primary Leadership Development Course) to Ranger School." While DeVos and the company commanders stayed on top of Ranger School volunteers, the CSM made sure each NCO was doing everything necessary to prepare himself for his next promotion. Part of this preparation included inspecting each NCO's official photograph to make sure it met the CSM's standards. Those standards were high. Very high.

As a young soldier, he was assigned to the "Old Guard," the 3rd Infantry Regiment, the unit who, among other things, is the major player in all of the ceremonial functions at Arlington National Cemetery. During his first assignment there as a young soldier, CSM DeYampert was one of those who guarded The Tomb of the Unknown Soldier. After a tour in Vietnam, he returned to the "Old Guard." This time he was an NCO who supervised the changing of the guards at the Tomb. On his third tour, as a SFC, he was the NCO assisting the President of the United States at the wreath laying ceremony at the Tomb of the Unknown Soldier on Memorial Day. As Susan DeVos said on more than once occasion, the CSM did not march like the rest of the soldiers. He glided. He was so smooth his feet never touched the ground.

The relationship between DeVos and CSM DeYampert was special, a bond between two professional soldiers. Like all good CSMs, CSM DeYampert was his battalion commander's confidant; a teacher; a voice of reason in the midst of chaos. And, if required, he was there to help keep his battalion commander from "stepping on some landmines."

One day as the two of them were walking toward the mess hall for their after-PT breakfast, DeVos noticed a soldier who appeared to be battered and bruised. He asked the CSM, "What happened to _____?" to which the CSM replied, "You really don't want to know." Ed thought about that briefly and then said, "Thank you, Sergeant Major" as they continued their walk to the mess hall.

One of the advantages of a COHORT unit is that because these soldiers know they will be together for up to three years, they tend to police themselves, meaning that if one member of a squad is not carrying his weight, his squad members may "counsel" the offender in rather harsh ways to inspire this wayward individual to shape up and become a team player. Sometimes this "counseling" can take on a more physical aspect to get the point across. If DeVos had started asking questions about the bruised soldier, he could put himself into a position of having to adjudicate on a matter that was already being addressed by members of that soldier's squad.

On several occasions when DeVos was "highly displeased" with one of his company commanders, rather than chewing the officer out himself, Ed dispatched the CSM to go and counsel the officer about his transgressions and why "the old man" was so ticked off.

One day as the two men happened upon of group of lieutenants, DeVos decided to use this opportunity to teach a short tactics class on "x" or "y" or "z." As the two walked away from this small group, the CSM said, "They didn't understand a thing you said." DeVos looked at the man. "What do you mean? I was good." The CSM response was quick, yet pointed. "Yeah, you were good for a colonel, but they're lieutenants. They don't have the background to understand what you were trying to tell 'em." An invaluable lesson, one that is similar to advice Abraham Lincoln gave to a young lawyer many years before. "When you're talking, don't shoot too high—aim lower and the common man will understand you."

* * * * *

Once the battalion leadership team was in place, there were minimal changes at first. Then over time, lieutenants were moved about some, but these moves were planned to develop the officers' potential for advancement later in their careers. It also helped that because of the emphasis on schooling, other soldiers gained valuable experience as they filled in the leadership gaps for those who were TDY, thus creating a win-win scenario which produced a stable full of rising stars throughout the organization.

Before leaving the topic of organization in 1-87 Infantry, it should be noted that the battalion under DeVos' direction did next to nothing unless it had a direct correlation to the battalion's goal of being one of the best infantry battalions in the Army. No time was spent on writing out a unit garrison SOP (Standard Operating Procedures) or a Field SOP as there were enough Army regulations and field manuals that covered all those necessary subjects. No time was spent sprucing up the battalion's World War II buildings with paint or plants to improve their appearance. No rocks were painted to outline walkways in the battalion area. No parking areas were lined with rocks or painted so that the soldiers' vehicles would be lined up dress right dress. When a division staff officer who was the same rank as DeVos called him one day to ask why so few of his officers were members of the officer's club, Ed asked the officer what did officer's club membership have to do with the battalion's mission. When that question was not answered to Ed's satisfaction, the call ended. It should be noted that DeVos was never asked about officer club membership by either General Carpenter or Colonel Keane. These two men were Infantrymen of the highest order and it seemed as though the priorities of these men were similar to Ed's. It was an honor to serve with them.

* * * * *

Training. During the train-up period before activation, DeVos gave his training brief to MG Carpenter and Colonel Keane and the other members of their leadership teams. It was short and to the point. After stating the battalion's goal, Ed used his only chart to describe how the battalion planned to achieve it. This chart looked much like the Dow Jones Industrial average which showed that while the lines went up and down daily, in the long run, the overall trend was always up and up, ending at the top right corner of the chart. The bottom left of the chart was activation day (May 1987); the top right corner was May 1989. As the battalion commander explained, during the unit's path to be the best, the battalion would have some good days and some not-so-good days, but as the battalion leadership and its soldiers learned from their mistakes, the battalion would get better and better as the "mountains" they were climbing were taller and taller.

After asking a few questions about specific dates and where DeVos expected to be at those points in time, the CG leaned back in his chair. "I got it. I've never seen a chart like that before but I got it. It paints a realistic picture. I look forward to watching this battalion grow." And out the door he went. DeVos continued to use that same chart at every quarterly training briefing from then on. The track shown on that original chart pretty much mirrored reality as the months passed.

As soon as the activation ceremonies were in the rear-view mirror, the serious work of molding these new infantry soldiers into professionals began. PT was first on the agenda. Every day, regardless of the weather conditions, which can produce snow in Northern New York from late September through early May, the soldiers of 1-87 Infantry did PT—seventy degrees in rain on a balmy day in June or minus twenty degrees in January. It made no difference because infantry soldiers must have the mind-set to be able to close with and destroy the enemy in all types of weather and in all types of terrain. It also helped to have one building in the battalion area filled with twelve Nautilus exercise machines which were available to the soldiers twenty- four hours a day. When in garrison, it was not unusual for platoons in the battalion to use this equipment twice a day. At each monthly gathering at the post theater, those members of the battalion who qualified to receive the expert physical fitness badge were singled out and presented their patch, which was then sewn on their black sweats, inspiring others to meet the same standards.

Every other week, unless the battalion was deployed off post, 1-87 Infantry would road march out to the training area on Monday night, train from Tuesday morning through late Thursday afternoon, and then road march back into garrison to arrive at dawn on Friday morning where the mess hall greeted them with a hot breakfast. Normally the road marches both out and in were between eighteen and twenty-five miles each way, depending on which training area the battalion used.

To DeVos, these road marches were a combination of four very important aspects of being a light infantryman. First was the physical fitness required by each soldier to carry a fifty to sixty pound rucksack on his back for long distances. Second, unlike their mechanized, airmobile, or airborne infantry brothers, light infantrymen go to war on their feet. It has been that way since Julius Caesar was a corporal and it will always be the Infantryman's primary means of transportation. There is only one way to toughen up the feet and that is you walk and then walk some more. Third, there are no restrictions as to when or where a soldier can road march as this can be done day or night and in all types of weather and terrain. From thirty-five below zero to one hundred degrees above, in torrential rains to desert sands, up the steepest mountains to the nastiest and densest swamps. And fourth, extended road marches in any and all types of weather and environments helped develop mental toughness in these men, teaching them they could go farther and faster than anyone else they would face on the battlefield. Much of the battalion's later success can be attributed to these road marches.

Whenever a soldier of 1-87 Infantry made his way into the maneuver areas of Fort Drum, he was in full combat gear and camouflage. During the first few months, the infantry companies' emphasis was on individual, then buddy team, and then squad fire and movement drills. These drills started with a walk-through, then at a quicker pace firing blanks, then live fire at a slow pace, and then live fire at a combat pace. Once the soldiers mastered these drills, then the same sequence was used at the squad level. To DeVos, the path to being the best infantry battalion was simple. Have the best infantry squads in the Army. That is where battles are won and lost.

All of this was to emphasize the critical nature of the last one hundred yards when the infantryman closes with and destroys the enemy. As the drills improved, each rifleman went through these live fires with fixed bayonets. Then these same drills were done at night. The sequence was always the same—walk through, run through with blanks, walk through live fire, then at combat speed live fire. Then the squads moved on to clearing a trench line with the same training sequence. The company commanders then began to add new wrinkles to these drills, showing their creativity and their confidence in their platoon and squad leaders, adding covering fire with M-60 machine guns and letting the soldiers use hand grenades to help clear the objectives. To show his confidence in his company commanders, when his companies were running their own live fire drills, DeVos told his company commanders he would not be present on the first day of their training because they were Infantry captains and he trusted them to get the kinks out and to do it right…crawl, walk, run. While the other battalion commanders thought DeVos was "betting his career" by not being present on the "first" day of these live fires, he never wavered. The trust that this established between Ed and his company commanders was too valuable. Captains like Pete Dillon, Rich Brewer, Terry Earnst, Tony Hammond, Dan Fitzgerald, Ashley Garman, David Gexler, and John O'Keeffe and their First Sergeants—Luis Bayrom, Seawal Hutchins, Dean Jackson, and Franklin Hance grabbed hold of the Light Infantry concepts and ran with them, far-exceeding expectations.

From the battalion's leadership perspective, as the soldiers became more accustomed to the smell and sounds of battle, "we" were well on our way to achieving "our" goal. Later, platoon and company fire and movement to contact exercises were held in the largest maneuver areas on Fort Drum, and when the battalion ran these, mortars, field artillery, and close air support from A-10 Warthogs were added. Before any of these went "live fire," the battalion followed the same sequence of training that was started at the individual and buddy team level.

The first test on the battalion's way to being the best was evaluated by MG Carpenter, Colonel Keane, and others in an early October 1987 exercise where 1-87 Infantry was pitted against another battalion. While the squads, platoons, and companies performed well, the exercise showed several "holes" in staff coordination which DeVos felt he should have anticipated. While the overall grade for the battalion in this test was excellent, Ed put his staff through some drills the following week to correct the shortfalls. With that test beyond them, the battalion was on the glide path of his chart shown to the CG four or five months earlier.

Soon after that, DeVos and many of his officers were given the task of helping evaluate another one of the division's light infantry battalions. This unit was part of the Division's 2nd Brigade which was stationed initially at Fort Benning and was now being moved to Fort Drum as facilities became available. Because this unit had done all of its train-up and initial training at Fort Benning, the harshness of Fort Drum's weather and terrain, coupled with some internal factors proved to be a challenge for this battalion. Near the end of the five day "test," MG Carpenter, a man who had been awarded a Distinguished Service Cross in Vietnam, asked Ed what he thought. After unsuccessfully dodging the question, DeVos stated that, right now, he would not want this battalion on his flank. The CG nodded. One month later that unit retook their "test."

* * * * *

It was around this time that DeVos had the worst day of his seventy-three hundred days in the Army. Early one evening, Ed had just gotten home from the battalion when he received a phone call from the battalion duty officer. The wife of one of his NCOs and their two sons had been involved in a serious automobile accident. Not knowing any of the specifics, Ed instructed the duty officer to contact the SFC's unit which was in the field and have them transport him immediately to the

Watertown hospital. After he hung up the phone, Ed and Susan headed there.

Once at the hospital and getting the details from the highway patrol, all Ed could do was wait. As he sat in the hallway just outside the emergency room, he prayed, and then prayed, and prayed some more. After what seemed like an eternity, the sergeant walked through the emergency room door. When the NCO saw Ed, he made a beeline for him. The first words out of his mouth were, "Who was it? Who died?'

It took DeVos a moment before he could get the words out. "Both boys. Your wife is hurt but she'll be OK." He then guided the soldier down the hallway to where his wife was being cared for. The wife was driving her two teenage boys to hockey practice late that afternoon. The weather was not the best. A man barreled through a stop sign at an intersection of two rural roads and hit her car broadside. The two boys, thirteen and eleven, died at the scene. The injuries to the sergeant's wife were not life threatening.

* * * * *

Deployments. After getting their "seal of approval" in the October 1987 "test," for the remainder of the time DeVos commanded 1-87 Infantry, there were deployments after deployments. When the battalion was at Fort Drum, the training cycle of going to the field on Monday nights and returning Friday mornings continued, but it was backed down to once every three weeks instead of every other week. The soldiers and their leaders needed time to recharge. It was a marathon, not a series of one-hundred-yard dashes. It was around this time that each company spent a week in Jericho, Vermont at Mountain Warfare School at Camp Ethan Allen.

During those close-to-home weeks, Ed spent many nights walking with squads as they conducted night ambushes. The overall thrust of the battalion at this point was that "we own the night." The recon platoon, in particular, prided itself on being able to move around at night at greater and greater distances and not be spotted, all while providing the battalion commander with valuable information. It helped as the number of Rangers in that platoon increased from three to eight in the first year from activation, and then swelled to twelve the next year. As one would expect, those areas needing correction that were identified on the battalion deployments went to the front of the line for training.

* * * * *

The battalion's first deployment was to Fort Bragg where the battalion went through a week of MOUT (Military Operations in Urban Terrain) training, a very difficult tactical environment where every door and every window can conceal an enemy, as Fort Drum did not have a training site like that. The weather at Fort Bragg in December 1987 was a comfortable forty degrees. While there, 1-87 Infantry soldiers wore their black tee shirts and shorts for PT. Members of the 82nd Airborne Division wore several layers of cold weather gear.

The next deployment a month later was to Fort Pickett near Blackstone, Virginia. This was a large training area used initially in World War II, but in the 1990s, this installation was deactivated because of the Base Reduction and Alignments. For one week the battalion had the run of the post doing its regular fire and maneuver drills on some unfamiliar ground and using the MOUT training learned at Fort Bragg to run company size exercises at Fort Pickett's smaller MOUT complex. It was a good week to be in Virginia because temperatures at Fort Drum dropped to thirty below that week.

April and May 1988 were a whirlwind—three exercises/deployments, one right after the other. As DeVos explained to the battalion's soldiers at the monthly payday briefing at the post theater in February, each of these upcoming exercises was going to be interesting. The first would be against 1-22 Infantry, a sister battalion in the 1st Brigade. Since each battalion was the same size, each knew the Fort Drum turf, and 1-22 Infantry was a "year older," this would be a heavyweight fight between two equally talented units. The second "fight" would be back at Fort Pickett two weeks later when 1-87 Infantry would go against two infantry battalions from the 82nd Airborne Division. DeVos told the battalion that day that it would be two against one. "We" are the one, but because each Light Fighter is equal to two paratroopers, we know the ground at Fort Pickett, and "we own the night," it would be a fairly even fight.

If the odds makers had put even odds on these exercises, they would have lost money on each of these bouts as the 1-87 Infantry soldiers showed their will and skill against these two worthy adversaries. Truth be told, the 1-87 Infantry versus the 1-22 Infantry bout was much closer than the one featuring 1-87 Infantry versus the two battalions from the 82nd Airborne Division. DeVos' assessment of that second exercise validated what he had learned sixteen, seventeen years before. Because airborne units have to spend precious time preparing for their airborne missions and contingencies, that takes away from the time they have to conduct all the training they needed to be successful against a skilled light infantry unit which doesn't have to be concerned about jumping out of airplanes.

The third in this series of exercises was back at Fort Drum three weeks after the Fort Pickett exercise. It was 1-87 Infantry against a National Guard Division of six infantry battalions. DeVos told his men, this still favored 1-87 Infantry: home turf, tougher and more physically fit soldiers, night operations, and the battalion was bubbling with confidence because of its last two "fights."

Less than a week before the exercise was to take place, DeVos was told he would have to come up with umpires for this exercise. During a quick meeting later that day, one of Ed's officers recommended that the battalion, each company, and each platoon conduct a fall-out-one-drill, meaning the XOs and platoon sergeants would command their respective unit while the normal leaders would be the umpires. This would solve the umpire issue and give each XO at the battalion and company level an opportunity to show their stuff as they commanded these organizations, and each platoon sergeant would run his platoon. It would also mean that it would be a fairer fight with the National Guard Division. This was a good example of how much better a unit can be if you get all the brain power in it working together. After hearing from the other leaders at the table, DeVos made the decision to follow this one officer's recommendation and it was so ordered. Yes, all objectives of the exercise were met and the "home team" won again.

In the summer of 1988 as the 10th Infantry Division matured, it, too, became subject to the same requirements as the 7th Infantry Division had gone through in terms of preparation for having a battalion ready to deploy in an eighteen-hour window. Therefore, the division adopted the DRF and DRB scheduling. During the set-up of this system, 1-87 Infantry was well-down the line to deploy and so the unit was able to be quite liberal in taking some time off and do some catch up with the families.

While all the activity of the last year plus had taken its toll, Ed's family under Susan's organized direction had adjusted well to the area and the Watertown schools. Both Kristen and Keith were heavy into sports and academics, and along with the other kids from military families in the local school systems, the contributions these families made throughout this part of upstate New York were beneficial for all concerned. It was good to get away for a week on a family vacation to Peak's Island, a short ferry ride from Portland, Maine, right on the Atlantic Ocean. The kids were also able to spend a week at sports camps that summer: Kristen at a volleyball camp and Keith at a basketball camp.

*****

As the short summer drew to a close, 1-87 Infantry found itself back on DRF1 and rumors began to float around. While the deployments of the 7th LID Ed had been a part of in both Korea and at the NTC had proven the value of the light infantry, there were some senior officers of the mechanized and armor forces in Europe who had their doubts. While there was no official announcement, there were many indicators that suggested that 1-87 Infantry would be alerted while it was on DRF1 and deploy to Germany in an EDRE (Emergency Deployment Readiness Exercise) as part of Reforger '88. This deployment, if it happened, would be similar to the 2-32 Infantry deployment into Korea in '85 Team Spirit.

As predicted, the alert came and the deployment to be "wheels up" from the departure airfield in eighteen hours was accomplished as planned. When the battalion arrived at an airfield in Germany, it was hustled onto C-130s, landing on a dirt strip near where it began to prepare to meet the opposing force as it came toward a high piece of critical terrain.

From alert notification to the battalion's soldiers digging the first foxholes in Germany was thirty-two hours. 1-87 Infantry's plan put its recon platoon on the first airplane, so once they landed in the maneuver area, these soldiers moved forward and began to provide DeVos with some real time information about the opposing force which enabled the battalion to make some adjustments to its initial battle plan. These adjustments allowed the battalion to fight the "enemy" mechanized units in depth on terrain favorable to the infantry. As was addressed in an earlier chapter, getting eyes on the ground is always favorable to a map or a visual recon from the air.

After stopping the enemy force at this first location, a day later, 1-87 Infantry was given a mission at 1100 to secure a critical road junction that was on the opposing force's Main Supply Route (MSR). The road junction, behind "enemy lines," was twenty miles away and consisted of five roads intersecting at this one road junction. The battalion's mission was to secure this key road intersection not later than (NLT) 0600 the next morning. Said another way, the battalion had nineteen hours to plan the mission, move twenty miles through enemy lines, and secure this piece of critical real estate against an unknown size enemy force. Warning orders were given, and planning started immediately.

* * * * *

Three days later, two days after the exercise had ended, the general officers of the major units that had participated in Reforger '88 gathered in a large conference room to conduct an after- action review of the exercise. Also in attendance was the commander of the 1st Brigade 10th Mountain Division, Col "Wolf" Kutter who had replaced Col Keane four months earlier, and LTC Ed DeVos, battalion commander of 1-87 Infantry. After discussing the first part of the exercise, attention turned to the last two days where the units that played the role of the opposing forces explained how their plans had ground to a halt because they had to deal with some infantry soldiers who would not budge off one major hilltop and then some more infantrymen seemed to appear out of nowhere and clogged up their MSR early the next day.

DeVos was then called on to briefly discuss the defense in depth of the key hill and then how his light infantry soldiers were able to move undetected behind the "enemy" lines to disrupt (virtually close down) the MSR so effectively. His explanation of squads being capable of infiltrating over such distances at night within company avenues of approach caught many senior officers flat-footed as they began to see the capabilities of the light infantry with new respect. While some could not understand how one unit could be so disruptive, evaluators who accompanied elements of the battalion verified the movements and the veracity about how 1-87 Infantry accomplished its mission. Senior leadership was also astounded to learn that with the exception of each company contacting battalion by radio as phase lines were crossed, the movement was completed on radio silence, helping to insure the element of surprise.

What DeVos did not tell these generals was that this was the first time the battalion had ever infiltrated the entire battalion at one time. It had been practiced at the company level before, so it was just a matter of assigning each company an avenue of approach and staying out of their way. After the briefing was over, Col Kutter and DeVos received a number of "well-done" by those officers who attended the briefing.

That night at dinner, Ed told Col Kutter he had talked recently to Infantry Branch prior to this deployment and they indicated after his battalion command time ended in May 1989, he would most likely be going to the War College for a year and then to the Pentagon for a year or two, which would then put him in line to command a brigade at some unknown location, but of course, there were no guarantees. Promotion to Colonel was pretty much a lock.

Ed went on to tell "Wolf" that, considering that information and realizing he was now in the best job he could ever have in the Army, he and Susan were seriously considering retiring from the Army right after he changed command as that would coincide with his twenty years in the service. Facts weighing in on this decision were that for the last five plus years, he had lived a dream—being with light infantry soldiers literally from the ground up from the first hand-drawn chart he had given to General Moore. He had been on more deployments, exercises, and live fires than he could count. And he had been with the best soldiers he could ever imagine.

While the family had never complained, since his next assignments would take him away from soldiers without any guarantee that he would ever be back with them, it was time to put the family first. They had paid a heavy price for this wonderful ride he had been on.

* * * * *

Once the battalion reaturned from Germany and after receiving a number of accolades, it was time to go back to work. More deployments.

First there was a company-size deployment to the NTC at Fort Irwin where one of the battalion's rifle companies was part of the OPFOR going against a mechanized/armored heavy unit. Taking advantage of stealth and the night, this infantry company proved once again that light infantry soldiers can provide a new dimension to the battlefield. During his two days look-see, Ed met the famed author Tom Clancy who was doing some research for one of his next books. He was a bit gruff but who isn't at 0200 in the morning. Right behind this was another company deployment, this one to Camp Shelby, Mississippi. Just as Ed had experienced when he was a company commander at Fort Benning, these were times for these captains to be away from the flagpole on their own for periods of growth and confidence building.

In late February 1989, 1-87 Infantry deployed to Panama where the battalion went through JOTC, Jungle Operations Training Course. The soldiers had a great time, one that was talked about for months.

For Ed it was a time of reflection; a time to look back at this incredible journey these men had begun together in September 1986 and to think about their contributions that helped make the unit's success possible.

The first group DeVos thought about were those who were there at the ground floor in September and October 1986: Captains Nencho Kolev and Dan Ammerman, who took charge of all the administrative and logistics that were required to set up the unit areas, the mess hall, obtain all the equipment and weapons into the unit. Then there was Major John Harrington, the battalion's first operations officer who was on top of integration of the COHORT soldiers and the activation ceremony and all the activities that surrounded it. Simultaneously, he provided over-watch for the battalion's training that immediately followed that ceremony to prepare for the battalion's initial evaluation exercise held in October 1987.

Next Ed thought about the lieutenants who had to put their heart and souls into learning the business of leading Infantry platoons as they took the sage counsel of their company commanders and first sergeants and translated that into action. Men such as Mike Eggers, John Carpenter, Joe Merlo, Bernie Sparrow, John DeLoach, Dave Latham, Bruce Stanley, Dave Reid, Tito Martinez, and Todd McCaffrey who is still on active duty as a LTG, matured and went on to make significant contributions to the Army.

Then there was Major Rich Rowe, the battalion's second XO, who later retired as an MG and Major Steward Wade, the battalion's second S-3 who were steady rocks during the battalion's many deployments, to include REFORGER 88. In the background was Chief Warrant Officer Three (CWO-3) Jan Bond, the battalions' Physician's Assistant (PA) and medical platoon leader. He and his combat medics had a full-time job, healing untold numbers of strains and sprains, broken limbs, and going through vast amounts of ointments, mole skin, and medicines to relieve poison ivy, oak, and sumac, countless blisters, and other unknown aliments to keep all these five hundred light Infantrymen going strong.

Two others of special note were men of God. Chaplain Ken Sampson was a battalion chaplain in the 7th LID who was now a brigade chaplain at Fort Drum, and in that role he could always be found in the field "feeding his flock." Thanks to Ken, Chaplain Ed Ahl was assigned to be the Battalion Chaplain of 1-87 Infantry. A former Navy sailor, Ed was a man with unbounded energy who wanted to be with the soldiers, so much so, there were times he had to be held back from getting too far in front of live-fire exercises as it would have been very bad press to have a chaplain get shot on a training exercise. At last report, Ed, who now holds a PHD, is still counseling soldiers at Fort Bragg, NC.

And there was also some second-guessing on the decision he had made several months earlier when he had put in the paperwork to retire on 30 June 1989, two months after his change of command. The second-guessing part came because at the same time his retirement papers arrived in the Washington, D.C. area, news came from there telling him that he had been selected for Colonel, below the zone, meaning he was in the top one to two percent of his contemporaries. And he had been selected to attend the U.S. Army War College in August 1989. Who would be crazy enough to turn those opportunities down?

15. THE LAST FAREWELL

As DeVos considered that question over and over: Who would be crazy enough to...the answer was clear. The facts had not changed. At the battalion's change of command ceremony on 5 May 1989, he would be leaving soldiers, those wonderful Infantry soldiers. While some suggested he would surely get back to be with soldiers at some later date, there was no guarantee. Stuff happens. Most importantly and overriding it all was that he had given his word to Susan and to his family—he would be retiring and with a job opportunity in Watertown, the family would be stabilized there for some time, giving Keith the same opportunity that Kristen had—to stay at one location through his high school years. Ed could not go back on his word, regardless of the "carrots" that were dangled in front of him. It was an integrity issue. He had given his word. He said what he meant and meant what he said.

* * * * *

Between his change of command ceremony and his actual retirement from the Army, the Army Research Institute (ARI), the same organization which had captured a lot of data about him fifteen years earlier at Fort Benning, requested that he come to Washington D.C. for a day so they could ask him some questions. From what little they told him on the phone, they wanted to know how or why 1-87 Infantry had performed as it had. What caused this one battalion to be so different from so many others?

The meeting at ARI was much shorter than Ed expected as it seemed that the interviewers appeared to be looking for some great revelations or some magic potent that could be sprinkled on others to achieve better results. They wanted specifics of what the leadership climate in 1-87 Infantry was all about. Over the course of several hours, it seemed to DeVos that his responses were not what they were looking for. To help move things along, he gave them two examples of his style.

First, he told them that because of his experience in Infantry units, he was acutely aware of how his actions and reactions to the events of each day would affect all those around him because he knew that his officers and his NCOs would tend to mirror his reactions to the situations that would arise. In short, the morale of the unit hinged directly upon how he reacted to the events of the day. If he remained positive and upbeat, those around him would, for the most part, remain positive and upbeat as well. On the other hand, if he reacted negatively to a particular event, others would or could be caught up on his negative reaction. Therefore, because he embraced his role as the "chief morale officer" of the battalion, he always tried his best each day to remain positive and forward thinking, regardless of the events and trials that came his way.

Second, he explained to them he empowered as much responsibility as he could down to every leader in the battalion. One example he used had to do with Lieutenants being responsible for lieutenant "things." As DeVos explained to the interviewers, when an LT approached him with a LT problem, Ed would tell the LT that problem was below his pay grade as DeVos' job was to solve Lieutenant Colonel problems, not LT problems. And, if the LT could not solve his own problem, then he (the LT) needed to find other work. After addressing this issue in this manner several times, DeVos' pronouncement spread through the unit quickly, thereby insuring that each level of command took responsibility for their units.

When it appeared that Ed's responses were not going to help ARI find any quick solutions or any "silver bullets" or "pearls of wisdom," De-Vos gave them a copy of his leadership thoughts that he wrote out at the request of Chaplain Ken Sampson. Since this paper spelled out much of his leadership philosophy, DeVos thought these comments might provide ARI with some ideas they might wish to explore. These comments are shown below. It is interesting to note that Ed never heard another word from ARI after that meeting about this paper or anything else discussed that day.

"SPIRITUAL LEADERSHIP THOUGHTS"

1. There are four rules of success in the Army. Patience. Flexibility. Have a sense of humor. And keep your perspective.

2. Treat the other guy like you would like to be treated. Discipline with love, understanding, and empathy—but discipline nevertheless.

3. The only difference between a Colonel and a Private is time in service. Leaders should consider themselves to be caretakers, not rulers; big brothers, not demigods; stewards, not superiors.

4. When you are not in the field, you're not in the field. When you are in the field, you're working 24 hours a day, but in garrison, things should (can) get done in a timely manner.

5. Establish what is really important and then prioritize accordingly. Don't waste time on the unimportant things that no one really cares about. Keep focused on the mission of your unit.

6. A soldier has only one family. When there is a graduation, anniversary, etc. unless we are going to war, he should be with them.

7. Take time to THINK. Learn to put your feet up on the desk, lean back, and play "what if..."

8. What keeps (your) personal attitude up??? His eye is on the sparrow and I know He's watching me.

9. Share your thoughts, dreams, fears, etc. with others and they will probably share theirs with you. All of us like to know that there are others rowing alongside of us in this boat of life.

10. Trust is built over a long time. It is a long, hard, difficult accomplishment which can be torn (apart) with the whisper of a small voice.

11. While the truth and bad news may be painful, they do not get any better with time.

12. Rank does not follow you outside the gate when you retire. What you are looks back at you every day in the mirror. You can fool others, but you can't fool yourself (or God).

13. If life is too tough for you, consider the alternative. Then you may find life isn't so bad after all.

14. Everyone but the Chief of Staff of the Army will miss a list someday. Just because you spent a lot of time at work doesn't mean a thing.

15. All anyone can ask of you is to do your best. The question then is, "What is your best?" Can your best be improved? Will hard work and effort improve your best? Answer — Of course!!!

16. Do things because they are the right things to do, not because someone is coming to inspect, observe, or test you.

17. One of the definitions of the word "Lead" is to serve. Therefore, a leader is to serve others and not be served. Some leaders reverse the meaning.

18. The higher up the flag pole you climb, the more your ass shows.

19. Don't hesitate to explain *why* you are doing something or *why* something is important. If people know *why* they are doing something, they will be much more inclined to do the job well. If you leave them in the dark, you are getting what you asked for.

20. A simple "thank you" sincerely said or written goes a long way to cementing a relationship or bond between two people. Leaders should be especially mindful of saying "Thanks" since it is generally everyone else who does the work.

21. Subordinates want to know their leaders care, bleed, cry, have families, have feelings, experience love and hate, passion and fear. In other words, subordinates do not expect their leaders to be super human. On the contrary, they expect them to be nothing more than human. But very truthful humans.

22. To help keep your perspective, your first question in virtually every situation or crisis should be "Was anyone killed?" Once you know the answer to that question, you'll be able to look more objectively at the problem, situation, etc.

* * * * *

There were many times in Ed's life when he held back tears as he stood in front of soldiers: for what they meant to him, how he loved them, for who they were and what they had accomplished, how they had endured every challenge set before them, and how they so magnificently came through every mission with their heads held high and proud, humbling him with their desire and willingness to go do their job again and again.

There were two times in the summer of 1989 when he could not hold back his tears — tears of pride, tears of joy and sadness, tears of thankfulness that he had been privileged to be in the company of over five hundred men for the last two and a half years of his Army career, watching them grow and develop literally from the ground up.

The first was during the change of command of the 1st Battalion, 87th Infantry from DeVos to another outstanding infantry officer, and the second time was at his official retirement from the Army six weeks later. It was during this second ceremony that the tears flowed unashamedly for the unit that passed in review in front of him was once again the 1st Battalion, 87th Infantry. The Command Sergeant

Major of the battalion, CSM Eddie C. DeYampert (now deceased), requested that this battalion would pass in review for him and that the non-commissioned officers would be in charge of the formation. While these men had honored him with many gifts, the three he treasured above the rest were a hand carved walking stick, a plaque with the words—"Commander/Trainer/Mentor/Soldier. Our success is fruit of your professional leadership, your legacy is in the skill and will of our soldiers—The Army's future" fixed on it, and a life-size Expert Infantryman's Badge made of wood holding a fully capable rifle. To have these NCOs honor him in that farewell review is something he would never forget.

As these soldiers marched by the reviewing stand that dreary late June day, his mind raced through many of the events and people that had led to him receiving such a high honor.

Editor's comments: At his retirement ceremony, Lieutenant Colonel DeVos received the Legion of Merit, an award presented for exceptionally meritorious service. Part of that citation reads: "…As Battalion Commander of the 1st Battalion, 87th Infantry, (he) and his unit set the standard for all light infantry battalions…

* * * * *

In his book, *"Almost a Miracle," The American Victory in the War of Independence*, John Ferling quotes a Private Martin, a Revolutionary War soldier who, while on leave, discovered he missed his companions in the Army and so he wrote about them. "Me and my fellow soldiers had lived together as a family of brothers for several years, setting aside some little family squabbles, like most other families, had shared with each other the hardships, dangers, and sufferings incident to a soldier's life; had sympathized with each other in trouble and sickness; had assisted in bearing each other's burdens or strove to make them lighter by council and advice; had endeavored to conceal each other's faults or make them appear in as good a light as they would bear. In short, the soldiers, each in his particular circle of acquaintance, were a strict band of brothers ... faithful to each other."

EPILOGUE

Once I retired from the Army after a little over seventy-three hundred days on active duty, I have put my family in the front of the line, investing as much time as I can to repay them for all the opportunities they had given me to use my gifts and talents, doing what I loved.

Since the summer of 1989, God has continued to bless me. I was a very successful self-employed businessman in the financial services industry for over seventeen years, twelve years with a company that focused specifically on helping men and women who wore the uniforms of our country, and the last five years in a highly regarded company that served a broader clientele. I have been a part of several churches, serving as a Deacon and have been a Sunday School teacher for over twenty-five years. I have had the opportunity to serve the public as a member of a county's planning board for three years, been a poll worker during five election cycles, two of which were national elections, and served as a member of a grand jury for a year.

I have written four historical narratives about soldiers who exhibited courage and valor, integrity and honor, and have had the opportunity to speak several hundred times about those works and given remarks at various Vietnam and Memorial Day and Veterans Day events. I have also been the "Chaplain" of our local Military Officers of America Association (MOAA) for a number of years. And over the years I have contributed four articles that have been published in the *Infantry* magazine. A fifth one is pending.

These opportunities have come my way because of what I learned from so many others with whom I served.

* * * * *

I have many people to thank for their guidance, their support, their friendship, and their example of true professionalism on this journey I was privileged to take, and because it is a very long list, I know if I started to write down all who should be on that list, some names will be forgotten. Therefore, I beg your indulgence as I mention only five men: Command Sergeant Major Bill Edge (deceased) for his example of how a professional non-commissioned officer goes about his business; Major General Willard Latham, a man who never wavered from his convictions; Lieutenant General Jim Moore (deceased) who demonstrated compassion and care for all those around him; General Jack Keane, who in my view, focused on being the best Brigade Commander he could be rather than on future promotions; and Colonel Mike Malone (deceased), a warrior, teacher, author of a book titled, *Small Unit Leadership—A Commonsense Approach*, and my friend, who took me under his wing and was my sounding board the last five years of my career. Each of these men modeled how it is possible to accomplish the mission and take care of your men at the same time.

* * * * *

Like most who have served our country for any length of time, each of us has memories, lasting memories. Some of those memories make us laugh, some make us cry, some swell our chests with pride and some humble us, and some cause us to relive those times that will never leave us. These memories are part of who we are, what we think, what we believe, and what we cherish. So as I close, let me share some of my memories ...

I remember soldiers standing straight and tall, rock steady, eyes fixed, snapping to attention when that command was given. I remember watching the National and Unit colors dance in the wind on parade fields. I remember my heart stirring whenever "Taps" was played. I remember a man whose name I do not know at every POW MIA Remembrance Ceremony. I remember standing reverently at post theaters as the National Anthem was played before the movies.

I remember the crack of bullets, the mortar rounds whistling overhead, the screams of artillery, and the thud of bombs bursting nearby. I remember the calm reassuring voices of untold numbers of pilots who swooped down to bring hellfire and brimstone down on those who meant to do me and those with me great harm.

I remember the sound of airplane engines next to my ears just before leaping out into a pitch-black night from twelve hundred feet. I remember the sound of a distant Blackhawk helicopter inbound to pick me and those with me up at the edge of a forest at dawn, the snow around us crisp and sparkling in the twenty degrees below zero cold.

I remember nights moving through jungles so black you had to hold onto the gear of the man in front of you, hoping he will not trip or stumble. I remember on a still clear, black night in the high desert at Fort Irwin looking up to the heavens, finding myself incapable of counting all the stars God had placed over my head.

I remember watching an NCO instruct his soldiers on one of the many skills that would keep these men alive, sometimes using the soft voice of a teacher, and the next minute using more direct words of correction when one of these soldiers was not giving him his full attention.

I remember thanking God over and over for allowing me to be with such good men; men who each day were trying to do their best because they believed in themselves, in their fellow soldiers, in their leaders, and in their country. I remember the many times God kept me from harm, allowing me to return to the family that loved me.

I remember having the honor of leading my son, Keith, in his Oath of Enlistment as he joined the ranks of the Infantry. And I remember the slight, quiet nod or slight dip of the head one professional would give another, regardless of their ranks, to signify the recognition for a job well done.

* * * * *

And like so many of you, if I could, I would do it all over again.

I am the Infantry. Follow me.

ABBREVIATIONS

AAR — After Action review

AO — Area of Operation

APG — Aberdeen Proving Ground

ARI — Army Research Institute

ARVN — Army of South Vietnam

BG — Brigadier General (O-7) One star

"Black hats" — Airborne School Instructors

BOQ — Bachelor Officer Quarters

BRAC — Base Realignment and Closure

BSF — Bible Study Fellowship

CPT — Captain (O-3)

CENTAG — Central Army Group

CINCUSAEUR — Commander in Chief, United States Army, Europe

COHORT — Cohesion, operational readiness, and training

COL — Colonel (O-6)

CIB — Combat Infantryman's Badge

CG — Commanding General

CGSC — Command and General Staff College

CP — Command Post

CPX — Command Post exercise

C Rations — Basic ration for Soldiers in the field in Vietnam and Cold War era

CSA—Army Chief of Staff (O-10). Four stars

CSM—Command Sergeant Major (E-9)

CWO-3—Chief Warrant Officer Three

DA—Department of the Army

DMG—Distinguished Military Graduate

DRB—Division Ready Brigade

DRF—Division Ready Force

DZ—Drop Zone

FM—Field Manuel

FOSCOM—U.S. Army Forces Command

FSC—Florida Southern College

FTX—Field Training Exercises

Graf—Grafenwoehr, Germany. U.S. Army training area

Huey—UH1 Helicopter

HUMVEE—High mobility multipurpose wheeled vehicle

1LT—First Lieutenant (O-2)

IPR—In Process Review

1st Sgt—First Sergeant (E-8)

IOAC—Infantry Officer's Advance Course

IOBC—Infantry Officer's Basic Course

JOTC—Jungle Operations Training Course

KP—Kitchen Police

LID—Light Infantry Division

LTC—Lieutenant Colonel (O-5)

LTG—Lieutenant General (O-9) Three stars.

LZ—Landing Zone

MACSOG—Military Assistance Command Special Operations Group

MACV—Military Assistance Command, Vietnam

MAJ—Major (O-4)

MATA—Military Assistance Training for Advisors

MG—Major General (O-8) Two stars.

MMAS — Masters of Military Arts and Science
MOUT — Military Operations in Urbanized Terrain
MRE — Meals ready to eat
MSD — Minimum Safe Distance
MSI — First year ROTC Cadet, a freshman
MSII — Second year ROTC cadet, a sophomore
MSIII — Third Year ROTC cadet, a junior
MSIV — Fourth Year ROTC cadet, a senior
MSR — Main Supply Route
NCO — Non-Commissioned Officer
NLT — Not Later Than
NTC — National Training Center
NVA — North Vietnamese Army
OCF — Officer Christian Fellowship
OCS — Officer's Candidate School
OER — Officer Efficiency Report
OPCON — Operational Control
PCS — Permanent Change of Station
PA — Physician's Assistant
PLDC — Primary Leadership Development Course
PLEX — Plans and Exercises
PLF — Parachute Landing Fall
PMS — Professor of Military Science
PT — Physical Training
R & R — Rest and Recuperation
REFORGER — Return of Forces to Germany
RIF — Reduction In Force
RIs — Ranger Instructors
ROTC — Reserve Officers' Training Corp
SAMS — School of Advanced Military Studies
2LT — Second Lieutenant (O-1)

SFC—Sergeant First Class (E-7)
SSG—Staff Sergeant (E-6)
SOP—Standard Operating Procedures
TOC—Tactical Operations Center
TO&E—Table of Organization and Equipment
TDY—Temporary Duty Assignment
TKE—Tau Kappa Epsilon
TRADOC—Training and Doctrine Command
UCMJ—Uniform Code of Military Justice
USAREUR—United States Army, Europe
VC—Viet Cong
WEL—Weapons Effectiveness Laboratory
XO—Executive Officer

ABOUT THE AUTHOR

Ed DeVos, a highly decorated military officer, is an experienced writer of thought-provoking historical narratives. His previous works, The Stain, The Chaplain's Cross, Revenge at Kings Mountain, and Family of Warriors have all received outstanding reviews. The Last 100 Yards is about some of his experiences as an Infantry Soldier for over twenty years.

CPSIA information can be obtained
at www.ICGtesting.com
Printed in the USA
BVHW072246160522
637194BV00001B/73